THE KARMA OF VOCATION

THE KARMA OF VOCATION

Rudolf Steiner

ANTHROPOSOPHIC PRESS

Library of Congress Cataloging in Publication Data

Steiner, Rudolf, 1861–1925
  The Karma of Vocation.

"The ten lectures presented here were given in Dornach,
Switzerland, November 4 through 27, 1916. In the Collected
edition of Rudolf Steiner's works, the volume containing the
German texts is entitled *Das Karma des Berufes des Menschen
in Anknüpfung an Goethe's Leben* (vol. 172 in the Collected
edition). They were originally translated from the German
by Olin D. Wannamaker and revised for this edition by Gil-
bert Church, Ph.D. The final revision was prepared by Peter
Mollenhauer"—T.p. verso.
  Rev. ed. of: The karma of human vocation in connection
with the life of Goethe. 1st ed. 1944.
  Includes bibliographical references.
  1. Anthroposophy—Addresses, essays, lectures.
2. Karma—Addresses, essays, lectures. 3. Goethe,
Johann Wolfgang von, 1749–1832— Addresses, essays,
lectures. I. Mollenhauer, Peter. II. Title.
BP595.S8544813   1984   299'.935   84-2902
ISBN 0-88010-085-0
ISBN 0-88010-086-9 (pbk.)

First Edition 1944

Second Edition 1984

Cover design by Peter Stebbing

About the Publication of
Rudolf Steiner's Lectures

The works written and published by Rudolf Steiner (1861–1925) constitute the foundation of anthroposophically oriented spiritual science. From 1900 to 1924, however, Steiner also gave a number of lectures and courses to the general public and to members of the Theosophical (later the Anthroposophical) Society. At first, he himself expressed the wish not to have his lectures, which were always delivered in loose form from a few sketches, committed to paper since they were "oral communications and not intended for publication." However, after some of his listeners had increasingly prepared and circulated incomplete and erroneous written reports of these lectures, Steiner felt compelled to regulate these practices and entrusted Marie Steiner-von Sievers with the task. She had to choose stenographers, administer the reports and take care of the editing for publication. Since Rudolf Steiner did not, except in a few isolated cases, have the time to correct the reports himself, his caveat regarding all publications of lectures must be taken into consideration: "What will have to be accepted, however, is that the transcriptions not checked by me may contain some errors."

In his autobiography, *The Course of My Life* (Chapter 35), Rudolf Steiner comments on the relationship of lectures for members, which initially were available only as internal printings of manuscripts, to his public writings. The exact text of these remarks can be found at the end of this volume. What is stated there is also applicable to the courses on special subject matters which addressed themselves to a limited circle of participants who were familiar with the foundations of spiritual science.

After the death of Marie Steiner (1867–1948), the publication of a complete edition of Rudolf Steiner's works was begun in accordance with her instructions. This volume is part of the complete edition. To the extent necessary, more information on the original texts is provided at the beginning of the "Footnotes."

Contents

I

Tomorrow I shall begin my discussion of the problems related to the connection of the spiritual scientific impulses with various unclarified tasks of the present time, and the influence that spiritual science must exert on individual, especially scientific, problems. Then I should like to refer to what I may call, in the sense of the fifth post-Atlantean cultural epoch, the karma of human vocation.

Today I shall take as my point of departure something that seemingly has little to do with that theme, but it will afford an opportunity to connect various related matters. I shall endeavor to point out the element in Goethe's life that characterizes him especially as a personality of the fifth post-Atlantean epoch, and much to which I have recently referred will, of course, be echoed in my remarks. I should like to bring before your souls the very facts pertaining to this personality that will enable anyone to distinguish important phenomena of the advancing post-Atlantean cultural epoch. In relation to the spiritual interests of humanity, the life and personality of Goethe are comprehensive and decisive to an extent that can hardly be ascribed to any other individual. Still, it may also be said that, in spite of much that has occurred, his life and personality have had the least possible effect on our lives. This, however, must be attributed to the very nature of our modern culture. It may be asked how it can possibly be said that the life of Goethe has remained without effect. Are not his works known? Has not an edition of his works, consisting of hundreds of volumes, been published recently? Did not his published letters number six or seven thousand by the turn of the century, and to-day number almost ten thousand? Is there not a wealth of literature concerning Goethe, one might almost say in every civilized language? Do not his works continue to be produced on stage? Is not his major work, *Faust*, brought again and again before the minds of men?

Now, I have often referred recently to the strange error of an illustrious contemporary scholar, which is really far more symptomatic of the character of our time than one might assume. A dominant scientist, this scholar speaks of the significance of the scientific world conception in such a way that he presents it as being the most brilliant, not only of our age, but of all ages in human history. He concludes that although it is hard to prove that we live in the best of all worlds, it is certain to the scientist, at least, that today we humans live in the best of all epochs, and we might exclaim in the words of Goethe:

'Tis delightful to transport
Oneself into the spirit of the past,
To see in times before us how a wise man thought,
And what a glorious height we have achieved at last.[1]*

This noted scientist[2] is gravely in error; he presents this as his own innermost sentiment and believes that he is thereby associating himself with Goethe, who is renowned for his knowledge of the world and of man. But he is really associating himself with Wagner, whom Goethe sets up as a foil to the Faust figure. Yet such a blunder contains at least a good bit of the honesty of our age because this person speaks more genuinely than the numerous people who, in quoting Goethe, have *Faust* on their tongues, but really have an undisguised Wagner attitude of mind. As a basis for

---

*Except when noted otherwise, quotations of Goethe's works are from translations by Ann Swanwick.

2

subsequent reflections, let us, then, bring up before our mind's eye the life of Goethe as a spiritual phenomenon.

If we wish to study human life in connection with the important question of destiny, if we study the questions of karma, we should remember that Goethe was born in a city and under conditions clearly of much meaning for his life. The family of Goethe's father had come to Frankfurt in the seventeenth century, whereas his mother's family, the Textors, was old, established, and highly respected, so much so that from it the mayors of Frankfurt were chosen. This fact alone signifies the respect enjoyed by the family at that time. Goethe's father was a man with an extraordinarily strong sense of duty, but for a man of his time, he also possessed a broad range of interests. He had traveled in Italy and representations of important Roman creations, about which he liked to talk, hung on all the walls of his Patrician Frankfurt home. What was dominant in the French culture of his time completely permeated the life of Frankfurt and most intimately influenced Goethe's home. The important world events were part of the life in his home, and his father took a deep interest in them. Goethe's mother, moreover, was a woman of the most spontaneous human sentiment, sharing directly in everything that connects human nature with the legendary, the fabulous, everything that lifts man aloft above the commonplace as if on the wings of poetic fantasy.

In Goethe's boyhood days it was much more possible to grow up unconfused by those disturbing influences that affect children today because they are dragged into school at a relatively early age. This did not happen to young Goethe; he developed extraordinarily freely in his parents' home under the austere but never harsh influence of his father and his poetically endowed mother. In later years he could recall with inner happiness these years of his boyhood and childhood that led to a ripe humanness. Many things that

3

we read today in Goethe's story of his life, *Poetry and Truth*, though decked out in a somewhat pedantic humor, have more meaning than may be supposed. In telling how he practiced the piano,[3] there is a profoundly human significance; the fingers of his hands, as if playing mythological roles, become soul-endowed, independent figures. They become Thumbling, Pointerling—I say this without sentimentality—and acquire certain mystical relations to the tones. This indicates how Goethe was to be guided into life as a complete human being. Not only a piece of this man, the head, should be guided, as so often happens, one-sidedly into life to be followed by the support of the rest of the body, developed through all sorts of athletics and sports; but, on the contrary, the body permeated by spirit to its very fingertips should be related with the outer world.

We must take into account from the very first the marked individuality of the innate endowments and nature of Goethe. From his earliest youth, everything pointed to a definite orientation of his life. As he grows in childhood, he is just as strongly inclined to follow with complete absorption the charming and stirring fairy tales and other narratives of his mother, thus even as a boy bringing his fantasy into living activity, as he is also inclined to escape from her and especially from his austere father. Slipping away into the narrow alleys, he would observe all sorts of things and also become entangled in varied situations through which he experienced in vital sentiments and emotions much that is stored up in human karma. His stern father guides the boy in a certain matter-of-fact way to what people in those days thought could provide support and direction in life. The father is a jurist who has grown up among, and is permeated with, Roman points of view; the son's soul, too, absorbs these views. In this process, however, through viewing the works and treasures of Roman art that represented what is essentially Roman, there was kindled in the boyish soul a

4

certain aspiration for what had been created in the culture of Rome.

Everything tended to situate Goethe in a quite definite way within the life of his time. In this way, he became, between the third and fourth centuries of the fifth post-Atlantean period, a personality bearing within him all the impulses of that period. Early on, he becomes a self-sustained personality, living out of his own nature, free of everything that binds a man in a fixed, pedantic way to those certain forms of one or another group of social ties. He learns to know social relationships in such a way that they affect him, but he is not united with them. He always keeps a certain isolated pedestal upon which he stands and from which he can establish connections with everything. From the very beginning, however, unlike so many others, he does not excessively identify himself with anything or with the environing circumstances. To be sure, all this results from a peculiarly favorable karma in which, when considered objectively, we shall find a solution for profound questions and problems regarding karma in general.

After Goethe had been introduced by his father to the field of jurisprudence, he was sent to the University of Leipzig, which he entered in 1765 at a relatively early age. We must not forget that when he joined this university life he was not tormented and exhausted by those strenuous exercises that must be suffered for an even longer period of time by young people in our day who are trying to pass the battery of final examinations at the conclusion of high school, the *Abitur*. After having passed their examinations, these young people are anxious to wipe the most recent learning experiences from their minds and enter a university in order to enjoy life. No, young Goethe had not entered the University of Leipzig simply to idle away his time but, nevertheless, he was not above skipping lectures and using the time saved for something else, as was done by many students. However, as he enlisted in the lofty and famous scientific life of the university, he came into circles that had never failed to awaken a longing in him whenever he had heard about them. Indeed, he knew above all that the famous Gottsched[4] worked at the university, Gottsched whose head held all the learning of the time and who expressed it in writing and orally to those associated with the contemporary culture of Leipzig. To be sure, Lessing's[5] great impulse was still to be felt in Leipzig, but it was natural for Goethe to think that the lofty Gottsched would introduce him to the entire scope of contemporary wisdom, enabling him to study conjointly jurisprudence and philosophy and whatever else a man of the world might derive from theology and learning regarding supernatural things.

Goethe, however, who possessed without doubt a certain sense for aesthetics, was slightly disillusioned when he first called on Gottsched. He appeared at Gottsched's door. I do not know whether or not the servant sensed something of Goethe's nature, but he admitted him directly into the presence of Gottsched without taking the time to announce him in the proper manner. So Goethe came upon the great man without his wig, standing there quite baldheaded. To a learned man in the year 1765 this was something quite dreadful. Goethe, who was sensitive to such things, had to witness how Gottsched seized his wig with a graceful turn and jammed it on his head, and how with his other hand he slapped his servant on the face. Goethe's enthusiasm was a little chilled. But he was still more chilled by the fact that Gottsched's entire demeanor corresponded little with that for which he longed.

Nor did Gellert's[6] moralistic lectures speak to him of the comprehensive intellectual horizons he desired. Therefore, he soon turned his attention more to the medical and scientific lectures, which were in a way continued in the home of Professor Ludwig, where he took his lunch and where much of a similar nature was discussed. It cannot really be said that Goethe "studied thoroughly jurisprudence, medicine, philosophy and, unfortunately, also theology"[7] in Leipzig, but he got a view of them and, most important, it was in Leipzig that he absorbed many a scientific concept of his time.

After having busied himself with the sciences, having experienced various aspects of life, and having been involved in various affairs, he then became so ill that he stood face to face with death. Such things must be taken fully into account by one who considers the human being in a spiritual scientific way. We must realize how much passed through his soul as he actually faced death because of extremely severe and recurring hemorrhaging. He was weakened, had to return home, and could not resume his university studies for some time.

When Goethe did continue his studies in Strassburg, he joined the circle of an important personality who became of exceptional significance to him. In order to judge with what feelings he met this personality, we must recall that, when he returned to Frankfurt under the influence of those inner experiences through which he had passed in Leipzig when he was face to face with death, he had already begun to enter more deeply, through association with various persons, into a mystical experience and a mystical conception of the world. He had immersed himself in mystic, occult writings and sought in a youthful way to elaborate a systematic world conception that took its point of departure in mystical—one might say, mystic-cabalistic—points of view. Even then he endeavored to learn "what secret force/ dwells in the world and rules its course"[8] and to open himself to the influence of "every working force and seed."[9] He was unwilling merely "to trade in words," as he had seen this done in Leipzig.

Then he came to Strassburg where he could again attend

lectures on science, and this is what he did at first. Jurisprudence, which was so dear to his father but less so to him, would be taken care of somehow, no doubt, but his most urgent impulse was to investigate how various laws of nature conform to one another. As he was once ascending a flight of stairs, he met a personality who immediately made a tremendous impression on him, not only through his external appearance, but also through an inner light that radiated through a highly intelligent countenance. Externally, a man approached him who had, indeed, somewhat the appearance of a priest, but who wore his long overcoat in such a curious way that the train was stuffed into his hind pockets. The man who made such a grand impression on Goethe was Herder.[10]

Goethe now entered vitally into all that then stirred tempestuously in Herder, and that was indeed a good deal. One might say that Herder bore within him an entirely new world conception. Basically, what had never before been undertaken, Herder bore it brilliantly within himself; that is, the endeavor to trace the phenomena of the world from the simplest entity, the simplest lifeless thing, through the plant world to the animal kingdom, on to man, to history, and even to the divine governance of the world in history. At that time, Herder's mind already harbored a vast, comprehensive view of the world, and he spoke with enthusiasm about his new ideas; but he also on occasion spoke with indignation against all pedantic, traditional ideas. Many of these conversations with Herder animated Goethe. That everything in the world is in process of evolution and that a spiritual plan of the universe sustains all evolution was a connection Herder perceived as no one ever had before. But this was still growing in him, and he had not yet expressed it on paper. Goethe received it in this state of being born and shared in Herder's aspiration, contemplation, and struggle. We may say that Herder wished to trace the evolution of the world from a grain of dust through all the kingdoms of nature up to God. He then did this in a splendid comprehensive fashion, as far as was necessary at that time, in his incomparable work, *Ideas for a Philosophy of Human History*. Here we can really see that Herder's mind grasped everything that was then known of the facts of nature and of the human realm, but all this knowledge was condensed into a world conception permeated with spirit.

Beside this, Goethe received through Herder an idea of Spinoza's contribution to the evolution of a new concept of the world, and this worked on him. The leaning that Goethe showed throughout his life toward Spinoza[11] was planted in him at that time in Strassburg by Herder.[12]

Herder was an enthusiastic admirer of Shakespeare,[13] which was something unheard of at that time. Just think how this peculiar polarity of souls must have worked between Herder and Goethe when Goethe, yearning to perceive these things that contemporary culture could not give him, found in Herder a revolutionary spirit of the first rank storming the culture of his day. Up to that time Goethe had learned to revere that art of form that is found in Corneille and Racine,[14] and had taken all this in as one takes in things that are said to be the most important in the world. But he had absorbed all this with a certain inner indignation. When Herder introduced him to Shakespeare, it worked on his mind like a breath of fresh air. Here was a poet free from everything formal—who created characters directly from human individualities; who possessed nothing of all the unity of time, place, and action that Goethe had learned to value so highly, but who presented human beings in his plays. We may say that a revolutionary cultural mood came to life in Goethe, now baptized in the name of Shakespeare, which we may express thus: I want to comprehend what constitutes the human being himself, not how he is put into the interrelationships of the world by formal rules and laws, or by the network of unities of situation, time, place, and action.

In this regard, he was able to become acquainted with men then in Strassburg who sought to look into the deeper and more intimate aspects of the life of the soul. One of them was the remarkable Jung-Stilling,[15] for example, who was studying the occult aspects of the life of the soul and knew how to describe them thoroughly. His life history, his description of what he calls the "gray man" who rules in the subterranean sphere of the earth, belongs among the finest descriptions of occult relationships. It may be said that Goethe was introduced by Herder to all that belongs to the life of nature and history, the aesthetic in life, and by Jung-Stilling to the occult aspects of human life, with which he had already familiarized himself in Frankfurt through an exhaustive study of Swedenborg.[16]

Such ideas fermented in Goethe's mind in connection with what had been passed on to him as the laws of nature while he was attending lectures on the sciences in Strassburg. Then he began to see the great problems and questions of human life. He looked deeply into what can be cognized and what can be willed by man, and into the relation between human nature and universal nature. Earlier in Frankfurt he had become acquainted with the work of Paracelsus[17] in connection with all this. And thus, a profound longing to perceive "every working force and seed" took a hold of him, especially in Strassburg along with all that he otherwise experienced there.

It must not be imagined that, in Strassburg, Goethe simply trifled away his time during his frequent visits to the pastor's home in Sesenheim,[18] although I certainly do not want to deprecate the importance of these visits. He was always capable of uniting life in the depths of man's will and cognition with life in association with the immediately human and ordinary, and with every human destiny.

10

After he had defended his dissertation, he became a sort of Doctor of Jurisprudence—Licentiate[19] and Doctor of Jurisprudence. He thereby satisfied his father and could return home. The practice of law began, but there was a notable disharmony in the soul of this man who had to study legal documents at the Supreme Court in Wetzlar that were often literally hundreds of years old. There "law and rights like an endless illness" dragged along their weary way. Even in later times much of this sort of thing could still be experienced elsewhere. In a place where I grew up—permit me to interject this—I was able to experience the following. In the 1870s when I was a boy, we once heard that a man was to be imprisoned—in the seventies! He was a much respected man who had a rather large business for such a place. He was imprisoned for a year and a half, I think, because in 1848 he had thrown stones at an inn during the revolution! The lawsuit had actually continued from 1848 when, as a young boy, this person had thrown stones at an inn, until his present age. In 1873 he was imprisoned for a year and a half. It was, perhaps, not so bad then as when Goethe studied the documents at the Supreme Court, but it was still bad enough.

Goethe's work gave his father immense pleasure, and he shared with counsel and help the problems Goethe had to solve with the dusty documents. This is not to say, however, that Goethe was lacking in skill as a lawyer. That was by no means the case. He made his contribution as an attorney and his work at that time belies the recurring belief that a great spirit, living in the world of ideals, must be deficient in practical life. He was not at all lacking as an attorney. When lawyers these days point to their busy schedules and call attention to the fact that they have no time to read Goethe's works, one should point out to them that Goethe was unquestionably just as good a lawyer as they. That can be documented, as can many things related to his work. But in addition to being just as practical as only a practical man can be, Goethe at this time also carried within him the idea for his book, *Götz von Berlichingen*.[20] Indeed, he bore within him the idea for his *Faust*, too, which had already emerged in Frankfurt from his scientific studies and later from his acquaintance with Herder and Jung-Stilling.

Götz von Berlichingen—Gottfried von Berlichingen—evidences at once, as Goethe forms it into a work of art, what his own nature really was. Goethe's way of being introduces a new element into the intellectual activity of humanity. As artist or poet, he cannot be compared with Dante, Homer, or Shakespeare. He stands in a different relationship to poetic creation, and this is bound up, in turn, with the way his mode of being relates to the age in which he lives. This age, as it was expressed in his immediate, and also in his more comprehensive, environment, did not permit such a spirit as his to blend wholly with the period. The life of the state that we today take for granted did not exist around him. After all, he lived in a region where certain territories had, to a high degree, taken on individual forms. How this came about is not important, but he did not live in a large state. No great all-encompassing conformity spread over the area where he lived and grew up. The life about him was not narrowly organized and thus he could experience it everywhere in its individual manifestations and simultaneously expose himself to its universal meaning. And this is what distinguishes Goethe from other poets.

One day a book came into his hands that is, indeed, badly written but that interested him immensely. It was *Autobiography of the Iron-handed Gottfried of Berlichingen*, which dealt with that strange individual who participated in so many events of the sixteenth century, but whose part in them was of such a peculiar nature. When we read this autobiography, we see how, under the Emperor Maximilian and Charles the Fifth, he came into contact with every possible kind of person and took part in every possible kind of quarrel and battle during the first half of the century.

His activities, however, always come about in such a way that he takes part in one event, is wholly involved in it and expresses himself completely therein. Then he becomes involved in another event in an entirely different role; he is drawn into that, fights for the most varied issues, and is later captured. After he has bound himself by an oath not to take any further part in quarrels and is thereby left at peace in his castle in middle South Germany, he becomes involved in the peasant uprising. All this, however, occurs in such a way that we see he is never forced by the events; but what holds these disparate episodes together is really his personality, the character of Gottfried himself. When one reads the autobiography of this man, I will not say that the events in which he is involved bore one to death, but we are not really interested in his quarrels and battles. Yet, in spite of all the boredom of the single events, we are always interested in his personality, so strong in character and so rich in content.

These traits, however, are just what attracted Goethe to Gottfried of Berlichingen. Thus, he could see the substance, the life, and the struggle of the sixteenth century concentrated in one personality as he could never otherwise have seen it. This was what he needed. To him, this meant taking up history and becoming acquainted with it. The way in which one or another historian, after having searched through attics and wastebaskets, telescopes together in a few "pragmatic maxims"[21] individual historical periods would certainly not have suited Goethe. But to see a man standing alive in the midst of it, to see reflected in a human soul what is otherwise not of special interest, this had some meaning for him. He took this tedious, badly written autobiography of Gottfried of Berlichingen, read it, and really changed its content remarkably little. For this reason, he called the first version of this drama, if we choose so to designate it, *The History of Gottfried of Berlichingen with the Iron Hand, Dramatized.* He did not use the term *drama,* but *dramatized.* He had really only dramatized the history of Gottfried of Berlichingen, but in such a way that the whole period became alive through this man. Bear in mind, it was the sixteenth century, the time of the dawn of the post-Atlantean epoch. Goethe perceived this time through the character of Gottfried of Berlichingen, the man who grew up in middle South Germany.

At that time a fragment of life had already passed through Goethe's mind that is historical but seen really within actual life, not in what is "historic." It would not have been possible for him then, with all those problems of humanity in his mind to which I have alluded, to take just any individual and dramatize his life according to history. However, to dramatize the stammering autobiography of a being who worked upon him with complete humanness in such a way that it would reflect the dramatic art as revealed to him through the reading of Shakespeare, that was something he could do. So he became known in certain circles that were interested in this sort of thing since he had lifted a fragment of the past, which was a book sealed with seven seals, into his own present world. Of course, just as little was then known about what Goethe disclosed by means of the badly written history of Gottfried of the Sixteenth Century as is known today by many a pastor about the supersensible life.

Goethe had taken hold of human life. He had to, since his life style was one that made him blend with life as it revealed itself directly to him. To be sure, he continued to stand on an isolated pedestal, but as life touched him, he became one with it.

Goethe was to be brought into union with life in still another way. There is little conception today of something that constituted a profound trait of the soul life in the so-

14

called cultured world surrounding Goethe. People had become bound, as it were, to what had come about since the sixteenth century. In public life, the laws and statutes had been handed down like an inherited disease,[22] but the souls of men were, nevertheless, touched in a certain way by what we recognize as the impulse of souls of the fifth post-Atlantean epoch. The result was that, for the most deeply endowed natures, a profound disharmony ensued between what they sensed within the soul and what took place in the external world. This, to be sure, led to a marked sentimentality in experience.

To sense as strongly as possible how wide the gulf was between the actual world and what a true and warm human soul could feel, to express this contrast with all possible emphasis, was felt by many to be a profound necessity. The eye was directed toward the life of the world in which various ranks of society and the people with their various interests lived. But they often had little soul contact with each other in this public life. Yet, when these human beings were alone, they sought for a special life of the soul existing apart from external life, and for them to be able to say to themselves that this external life was wholly unlike all that the soul would strive after and hope for was felt to be a great relief. To get into such a sentimental mood was a characteristic of the age. Life, as it was publicly manifest, was felt to be bad and defective. People strove to search for life where it had not been besmirched by indifferent public existence, and where they could really enter in a vital way into the silent working and weaving of the world of nature, the peaceful life of animals and plants.

From this a mood gradually arose that affected many cultured spirits. To be able to weep over the disharmonies of the world afforded a tremendous satisfaction. Those writers were especially honored whose works tended to induce a flood of tears to fall upon the pages that were being read. To

15

be unhappy constituted for many the very happiness for which they longed. Someone takes a walk in the forest; he then returns and, sitting quite still in his room, reflects: "How many, many little flowers and tiny worms that I did not notice and trod under foot have sacrificed their lives to this walk of mine!" Then he weeps hot tears into his handkerchief over the discord between nature and human life. Letters written to beloved friends who were as sentimental as the writer begin with such expressions as "Dearly beloved Friend," and this, too, is moistened by a tear that falls on the paper and hastens away with the letter as a precious testimony to the friend.

This life still permeated a large part of the cultured world in the second half of the eighteenth century. It also surrounded Goethe, and he had much understanding of it, for there was much truth in this feeling of the disharmony between the frequently unconscious or vague feelings of the soul and what was afforded by the outer world, and Goethe could feel the truth in it. In those days, the silent plan of life between souls was not at all similar to what took place in the world as a whole. He had to go through this because he could be, and needed to be, touched by everything. But, in his contact with these things, he had to draw health-giving forces from his inner self repeatedly.

And thus in his youthful novel *The Sorrows of Young Werther*, he wrote himself free of this whole temper of the age, which we call Siegwart,[23] or Werther, fever, and which had taken possession of a large part of educated society. In the figure of Werther he concealed to such a degree as to come near to suicide what he had shared of this sentimental mood and the disharmonies of the world. It is for this reason that he has Werther end his life through suicide. It is well to consider that, on the one hand, it was possible for Goethe to be bound up with everything in the souls of those about him, even though he was so firmly rooted in his own individuality. On the other hand, what he was writing about cleansed his soul and at the same time became a work of art. After he had finished *Werther*, he was completely cured of him, whereas in many cases other persons were only then possessed because through the influence of the *Werther*, Werther fever raged in the most widespread circles. Goethe, however, was cured.

In estimating such things, we must not overlook the fact that Goethe possessed a broad inner horizon so that he could, in a sense, live within himself in polaric contrasts. He went through the Werther sickness and wrote himself free of it through *The Sorrows of Young Werther*. Yet, there is truth in what he wrote to a friend at that time. He sketched a picture of his loftily sentimental mood, but also said there was a Goethe other than the suicidal Goethe who harbored thoughts of hanging himself and who entertained thoughts for which he ought to be hanged. There was also a carnival Goethe,[24] who could put on all sorts of masks and disguises, and this Goethe also really lived artistically. We need only allow the more or less fragmentary dramatic creations of that time, *Satyros* and *Pater Brey*, to work upon us, and we shall be able to sense the scope of his inner life: on the one hand, the sentimentality of *Werther*, on the other, the humor of the *Satyros* and *Pater Brey*.

Satyros, the deified forest devil who develops a veritable pantheism and does not enjoy the fruits of culture, wants to return to nature in genuine Rousseau fashion. Raw chestnuts—what a royal repast! Such is the ideal of Satyros. But he is really a philosopher of nature who is quite familiar with its secrets, and—if you will excuse me—he wins his followers especially among women, is deified, but finally behaves quite badly. Here all false yearning after authoritarian belief is ridiculed with immense humor. Then in *Pater Brey* we see the cult of false prophets play a part and, under the mask of holiness, do all kinds of things. This, indeed, is not ridi-

17

culed but objectively presented with much humor. Here Goethe is a humorist in the most vital sense—a blunt humorist, expressing it all from the same constitution of soul that created *Werther*. He was able to do this not because he was superficial but because he was profound enough to grasp the polarities of human life.

Especially the *Werther* book gained Goethe a far-reaching reputation. It became well-known rather early,[25] and it was really this work that led the Archduke of Weimar to take an interest in him. The *Gottfried of Berlichingen* made a decided impression, but not among those who then considered themselves capable of understanding culture, art, and poetry. "An abominable imitation of bad English works; a disgusting platitude," said an eminent man of the time about this book.[26]

It was in 1775 that Goethe was able to transfer his activities to a different field of operation, to Weimar. The Duke of Weimar[27] became acquainted with Goethe and called him there, where he became the minister of state.

Nowadays, after the event, people have the feeling that Goethe had already written the *Gottfried of Berlichingen, The Sorrows of Young Werther*, and even carried with him to Weimar a large part of his *Faust*; they see in all this his most important accomplishment. He himself did not consider them to be of first importance at that time, but they were only the scrapings of his life. The Duke, likewise, did not appoint him court poet, but minister of state, which caused the pedants in Weimar to be beside themselves with anger. The Duke had to address a sort of epistolary decree to his people in which he justified himself by saying that Goethe was in his eyes simply a greater man than the pedants. The fact that he was made minister of state without having been previously—what shall I say?—under-councillor and upper-councillor, required at least some justification from the Duke, and that is what he produced.

Goethe was by no means a bad statesman and performed his ministerial duties not as part time work, but as matters of first importance. He was a far better statesman than many a minister who was not a Goethe in our sense. Anyone who personally convinces himself—as I may say with all modesty that I have done—of the way in which he performed his ministerial obligations will know that he was an excellent minister for the Duchy of Sachsen-Weimar and was completely devoted to his duties. Being a minister was his chief occupation, and he achieved a good deal during his ten years in this capacity.

He had brought with him a part of his *Faust*, which is listed in the collected works under the delectable title, *The Primordial Faust (Ur-Faust)*. All that we might call the upward vision of Faust was already alive in this version. How directly had Faust been taken from the life that touches every human soul!

In Weimar it was evident again that Goethe could not be completely captured by his environment. We often become acquainted with persons who are, in greater or lesser degree, merely the exponents of their files. Goethe, however, was not merely the exponent of the numerous documents he drew up as a Weimar functionary. In addition, he acclimated himself to the conditions in Weimar and, even though he remained on his isolated pedestal, he was nevertheless touched by everything human. The immediately human took form with him as art. Thus we see how the character of a woman, Frau von Stein,[28] with whom he formed a friendship, became a life problem for him. It was fundamentally his immediate view of her character that was the cause of his dramatizing the figure of *Iphigenia*. He wished to put into artistic form what worked on him in the character of Frau von Stein, and the legend of Iphigenia was only the means for solving this life problem. The relationships at the Weimar court, his life with Duke Karl August,

19

whose character was so strangely endowed, his view of the fate of the Duchess, and other connected circumstances, all became problems to him. Life became a question. He again needed a subject in order to master these relationships in an artistic way, and to do so he took that of *Tasso*. It was, however, really the Weimar situation that he artistically mastered.

It is, of course, impossible to enter here into the many details of Goethe's mental life, yet I wish to place these facts before you in order that we may form a spiritual scientific contact with them as examples. Even in the most early period of his stay in Weimar, through the various circumstances into which he was brought, the possibility arose of deepening his studies in natural science by independent work. He continued his plant studies and began anatomical studies at the University of Jena. He endeavored in everything to confirm in detail the ideas of the universal interrelationships he had received from Herder. He wished to study the connections within the plant kingdom and what was spiritually alive in plants. He wished to hold the kinship among the animals before his mind and to find the path upward from them to man. He wished to study the idea of evolution in direct connection with actual natural objects. You see, Goethe had taken up Herder's great idea to study the evolutionary phrases of all entities, a unitary spiritual process of becoming. In this thought he and Herder then stood practically alone because those who dominated the intellectual life of the time thought quite otherwise; everything was pigeonholed.

All intellectual activity can be found to work in two polaric directions: toward separation and toward union. It was important for Goethe and Herder to bring unity into diversity and multiplicity; others were simply content with neat classifications and clever division. For these people, the problem was to show, for example, how man is distin-

20

guished from the animal. Man, it was said, has no intermaxillary bone in the upper jaw in which the incisors are rooted, but only a unitary jawbone; only the animals have an intermaxillary bone. Goethe was certainly not materialistically inclined, and he had no desire to establish materialism. The thought, however, that the inner harmony of nature could not be confirmed because of such a detail offended his intelligence. He therefore undertook to prove, in opposition to all scientific authorities, that man also has an intermaxillary bone, and he succeeded. He thus arrived at his first important scientific treatise entitled, *An Intermaxillary Bone Is to Be Ascribed to Man as Well as to the Animal.*[29] He had thereby introduced a single detail into the evolution of thought with which he opposed the entire scientific world, and which is now an obvious, undisputed truth.

Goethe appears, not as the poet of *Werther*, of *Gottfried*, and of *Faust*, or as the poet in whose head *Iphigenia* and *Tasso* came into being, but as one possessing a profound insight into the interrelationships of nature, so that he now studies and labors as a genuine research scientist. We have here, not a one-sided scientist, poet, or minister; he is a complete human being aspiring in all directions.

Goethe lived in Weimar for about ten years and then could no longer suppress his yearning to go to Italy. So in the late eighties he undertook a journey to Italy as if it were an escape. We must not forget that he then, for the first time, entered into situations that he had longed for and cherished from his earliest youth. This was his first introduction to the world at large; you must remember that he had never before seen any other large city except Frankfurt. We must also not forget that Rome was the first city through which he viewed the theater of world history. This must be included in his life and also that he felt the whole stream of life pulsating in Rome as it had risen in the fifth post-Atlantean epoch. Goethe united what then worked

21

upon him as world history with the comprehensive world conception germinating in his mind. He traced the idea throughout the multiplicity of forms of plants, stones, and animals he had compared, and now followed them over the Apennine peninsula. He endeavored to confirm the idea of the "archetypal plant" over the broadest area and was able to do so. Every stone and plant interested him. How the multifold comes into form as the unit, this he allowed to work upon him.

Goethe also exposed himself to the influence of the great works of art, which revealed to him ancient Hellenism in its last feeble outgrowth. As he directed his objective glance over the multiplicity of nature, so also could he feel in the depths of his soul all the intimacies of the great art of the Renaissance. One need only read the words he spoke upon viewing Raphael's *Saint Cecilia* in Bologna, how, as he looked at it, he experienced in a wonderfully profound and intense manner all those feelings that lead man out of the sensory world into the supersensible. One need only read in his *Journey to Italy* how, as he gradually deepened his ideas of nature, he sensed in the presence of works of art that man really creates such works only when art works creatively from the depths of life. Greek art, he said, now became clear to him: "I have an intimation that they proceed according to the same laws by which nature proceeds and which I am tracing,"[30] and "These lofty works of art, being also the highest works of nature, have been created by man according to true and natural laws. Everything arbitrary, all mere fancy, falls away; there is necessity, there is God."[31] So he wrote to his Weimar friends.

Goethe took into himself something stupendous, and what he had previously felt and surmised now took form. Scenes of great importance in his *Faust* were composed at this time in Rome. *Iphigenia* and *Tasso* had already been sketched and partly completed in Weimar. Now he rewrote

22

them in verse. As he exposed himself constantly to classic works of art, he was now able to find the classic style that he wished to pour into these works. This was a regeneration, an actual rebirth of the soul, that he experienced in Italy. Thus, something peculiar now took form in his soul. He sensed a profound contrast between the aspirations of his age in what he had observed in his environment and what he had learned to feel as the loftiest expression of the purely human.

Goethe returned to Weimar to the world where works had been produced that entranced everybody. Schiller's *The Robbers*,[32] Heinse's *Ardinghello*, and other such literary reproductions seemed to him barbaric stuff; they contradicted everything that was now rooted and living in his soul. He felt within like an utterly lonely person and had, indeed, been almost completely forgotten when a path was opened for the friendship with Schiller.[33] The approach was difficult because nothing was more repugnant to him when he first returned than Schiller's youthful works. But the two men discovered one another, and in such a way as to establish a bond of friendship almost without counterpart in history. They stimulated one another, and Hermann Grimm rightly remarks that in their relationship we have, not only Goethe plus Schiller, but Schiller plus Goethe as well.[34] Each became something different through the other; each enriched the other.

Profound, all-embracing human problems arose in the soul of Goethe and Schiller. What had to be resolved by the world in a political way—the vast problem of human freedom—was present before their minds as a spiritually human problem. Others gave much thought to the question of how an external institution that would guarantee man freedom in his life could be established in the world, but to Schiller the problem was: how does man find freedom within his own soul? He devoted himself to this problem in developing his unique work, *Letters Regarding the Aesthetic Education of Humanity*. For Schiller the question was how man guides his soul above himself, from the ordinary status of life to a higher status. Man stands, on the one hand, within sensory nature, said Schiller; on the other, he stands face to face with the realm of logic. In neither is he free. He becomes free when he enjoys and creates aesthetically, when his thoughts develop in such a way that they are under compulsion, not of logic, but of taste and inclination, and at the same time, free of the sensible. Schiller demanded a middle position.

These *Letters Regarding the Aesthetic Education of Humanity* of Schiller belong among mankind's most cultivated writings. But it was a question, a human riddle, that he and Goethe had faced in thought. Goethe could not penetrate this problem philosophically in abstract thoughts as Schiller had done. He had to attack it in a living way, and he resolved it comprehensively in his own way in the fairy tale of *The Green Snake and the Beautiful Lily*. When Schiller undertook to show philosophically how man ascends from ordinary life to a higher life, Goethe undertook to show in his fairy tale, through the interplay of spiritual forces in the human soul, how man evolves spiritually from an everyday soul life to a higher one. What Schiller brought to light in a philosophic, abstract way, Goethe presented it in a magnificent visible form in this fairy tale. This he attached to a description of external life in his novel-like piece *Conversations of German Emigrants*. There really came to life in the inspired friendship between Goethe and Schiller all that man proposes to himself in riddling questions about life, and that is related to Faust's explanation of why he turned to a magic interpretation of the world:

> [That I might]
> Her vital powers, her embryo seeds, survey,
> And fling the trade in empty words away.[35]

Whoever penetrates the intellectual exchanges between Goethe and Schiller and sees what at that time came to life in the spirit of these two men receives through it as yet unrecognized and unrealized spiritual treasure—a treasure which manifests the aspirations of the fifth post-Atlantean epoch in an extraordinary manner. The innermost concern of the two was manifested through the way in which Schiller undertook to solve the riddle of man philosophically in his *Aesthetic Letters*, the way Goethe addressed himself to the realm of color in order to oppose Newton, and the ways he depicts the evolution of the human soul in the fairy tale of *The Green Snake and the Beautiful Lily*. All this comprises comprehensive questions that were destined, it would seem, to be of vital concern to but a few people.

Even though we have wished thus far to touch only upon such facts as bear upon the life of Goethe, it must also be remarked that, although many people nowadays believe they are capable of speaking about him, for many this Goethe period belongs to the past and is a book sealed with seven seals. In a certain sense, we may really feel pleased when someone is quite honest about this. It was, of course, narrow-minded of the famous scientist Dubois-Reymond[36] to deliver his discourse *Goethe and No End*. The same man, a rector of a university, who had previously described the limitations of a knowledge of nature and had made so many remarkable physiological discoveries, delivered his discourse on *Goethe and No End*! His remarks were narrow-minded because they arose from the opinion: "Yes, so many people talk about one who, after all, was only a dilettante; Goethe, the universal dilettante, is forever the subject of discussion. But how much have we since acquired about which he was, of course, totally ignorant—the cell theory, for example, the theory of electricity and advances in physiology!" All that was present in Dubois-Reymond's mind. "What was Goethe in comparison? People talk about his *Faust* as if he had given us an ideal of humanity."

25

Dubois-Reymond cannot see that Goethe really did set before us an ideal for humanity. He asks: "Would it not have been better to make Faust greater than Goethe made him and more useful for humanity? Goethe places before us a wretched fellow"—Dubois-Reymond did not use this expression but what he says is approximately the same—"a wretched fellow who cannot even master his own inner problems. Then, if Faust had been a virtuous fellow, he would have married Gretchen instead of seducing her; he would have invented the electric generator and the air pump and have become a famous professor." He says quite literally that if Faust had been a decent man, he would have married Gretchen and not seduced her. He would have invented the generator and air pump and would have performed other services for humanity and not have become such a debauched genius who got involved in all sorts of spiritistic nonsense.

Such a rectoral address, heard at the close of the nineteenth century, was certainly narrow-minded. Yet at least it is honest. We could wish that such honesty might appear more often; it is delightful because it corresponds with the truth. Thrice mendacious, however, is much of the laudation for Goethe and *Faust* that is brought forth by people who are happy "only when they find earthworms." The quotations from Goethe that we often hear are really only spiritual earthworms even though they are Goethe's own words.

Precisely through the relationship of our time with such a spirit as Goethe's is it possible to study the deep untruth of the present age. Many people do nothing more than "trade in words,"[37] even trade in the very words of Goethe, whereas his world conception contains an element of everything that leads to and must come to birth in the future evolution of mankind. As we have already suggested, this element not only unites with spiritual science, but is by its very nature already tied to spiritual science.

II

Our real purpose in this lecture, as you already know from what has been said, is to lead the way to an understanding of the karma of the individual and, in a broader sense, the collective karma of our time. But even when we consider human life as it concerns single individuals, it is extraordinarily complicated, and we must follow many threads that link a man to the past and present worlds if we wish to answer questions regarding his destiny. This fact will, perhaps, explain to you the detour I am taking, although I really wish to discuss something that is close to every person. Goethe's life was important in world history, and I will associate reflections with it that are intended to light up each individual existence. His life, to be sure, is accessible to us in many details. Even though the destiny of each human life is far removed from the destined course of such an exemplary spirit in world history, it is possible for each of us to gain viewpoints from the contemplation of it. Therefore, let us not be annoyed if the connections with our special questions, which we shall gradually approach, are here somewhat expanded.

When people trace Goethe's life in the way many do who pretend to be his biographers, they fail altogether to observe how rash men are in their tendency to link cause and effect.

Scientists are constantly reminded nowadays that many blunders are due to the adoption of the principle, "After a thing, therefore because of that thing" (*post hoc, ergo propter hoc*); that is, because one thing follows another, it must, therefore, be an effect proceeding from its cause. This is refuted in the scientific sphere, but in the field of the observation of human life we have not yet come to reject this principle altogether. Certain uncivilized people belonging to the Kamchadales believe that the water wagtails or similar birds bring on springtime because spring follows their arrival. Such conclusions are frequently drawn when people say: A thing that follows another in time must derive from it as the effect from its cause. We learn from Goethe's own narrative, from the description of this life shining above ordinary humanity, that he had this father and that mother and that he experienced certain things in his youth. We then derive what he did later in life, which made him so important for humanity, from these youthful impressions according to the principle that, because one thing follows something else in time, it must proceed from it. That is no more intelligent than when the coming of spring is supposed to be brought on by the water wagtails.

In the scientific sphere, this superstition has been sharply reproved; in the sphere of spiritual science there is still need to do so. It is explained quite nicely, for instance, that at a rather youthful period while Goethe was still a boy and French officers were quartered in his father's house during the occupation of Frankfurt, he saw how the famous *Lieutenant du roi Thoranc*[38] directed theatrical productions and employed painters there. Goethe thus came into contact with painting and the art of the theater while scarcely more than a child. His later inclination to art is thus glibly traced to these youthful impressions. To be sure, in his case we see his foreordained karma clearly at work from his earliest youth. Is not an especially prominent trait in Goethe's life the way in which he unites his views of art, the world, and nature and has always behind his artistic fantasy the aspiration to know the truth in natural phenomena? Do we not see that a clearly prescribed karma leads the boy of six or seven to assemble minerals and geological material that he finds in his father's collections and place them on a music stand to make of them an altar to the great God of Nature? He then sets a candle on this altar made of natural objects and instead of producing a light in an ordinary, mechanical way, he lets the earliest rays of the morning sun pass through a magnifying glass to light the candle, kindling a flame to offer to the great God of Nature. How impressive and beautiful is this orientation of the mind to what lives and weaves as spirit in the phenomena of nature even in this boy of six or seven! Most certainly, this trait must have come from an original potentiality, if we choose to call it that, and not from the environment, and we see how what he brought into this incarnation worked with special force.

When we consider the time into which Goethe was born, we shall observe a remarkable harmony between his nature and contemporary events. In accordance with the present world conception, people are often inclined to say that what Goethe created—the *Faust* and other things that he did for the elevation and spiritual permeation of humanity—have come into existence simply because he produced them according to his talents. It is more difficult with the things he has given to humanity to prove that they cannot be bound up in this simple sense with his person. But, in reference to certain phenomena of existence, just consider how short-sighted many kinds of reflections are even though they are supposed to be fundamentally concerned with the truth. In my most recent book, *The Riddle of Man*,[39] you can find de la Mettrie's statement that Erasmus of Rotterdam and Fontenelle would have become entirely different human beings if only small particles in their brains had been different. According to this view, we must assume that nothing of all that they produced would exist if, as de la Mettrie[40] suggests, they had been fools instead of wise men because of a slightly different constitution of the brain.

Now, this does apply in a certain sense for the things

Erasmus and Fontenelle produced, but consider this question in relation to another case. Can you imagine, for instance, the development of modern humanity without the discovery of America? Think of all that has entered into the life of modern humanity through the discovery of America. Could a materialistic person assert that if Columbus's brain had been a little different he would have been a different sort of man, a fool, who then would not have discovered American? Certainly, this could be asserted, just as it can be said that Goethe would not have been Goethe, nor Fontenelle have been Fontenelle, nor Erasmus have been Erasmus if, for example, their mothers had suffered accidents so that their children would have been stillborn. But we can by no means suppose that America would never have been discovered if it had not been discovered by Columbus. You will find it rather self-evident that America would have been discovered even if Columbus had suffered from a brain defect.

So you will certainly have no doubt that the course of world events is one thing and the participation of an individual in these events another. You will have no doubt that these events summon those individualities who are especially fitted through their karma for whatever is demanded of them. With reference to America we can easily think through to this conclusion. But, for those whose vision penetrates more deeply, the same truth applies to the genesis of *Faust*. We should have to assume utter nonsense in the evolution of the world if we had to suppose that there would have been no necessity for the creation of such a poetical composition as the *Faust* even if what the materialists like to emphasize so much had actually occurred and a tile had fallen on Goethe's head when he was five, making him an imbecile. Anyone who traces the course of spiritual life through the decades preceding the time of Goethe will see that the *Faust* was really a demand of the age. Lessing, indeed, is the typical spirit who wished to create a *Faust*—in fact, actually wrote a fine scene. It was not merely Goethe's subjective needs that demanded the *Faust*, it was demanded by the age. With respect to the course of events in world history, the truth is that a relationship similar to that between Columbus and the discovery of America exists also between Goethe's creations and Goethe himself.

I have said that, if we observe the age into which Goethe was born, we note at once a certain harmony between the individuality of Goethe and his age when taken in the broadest sense of the term. Bear in mind that, in spite of all the dissimilarities between Goethe and Schiller, there is, nevertheless, something quite similar in them—not to mention other less important contemporaries. Consider, for example, how much is resplendent in both Goethe and Herder. But we can go much further. When we look at Goethe, it does not, perhaps, appear at once—we shall come back to this later—but, when we look at Schiller, at Herder and Lessing, we shall say that their lives were different, of course, but that in their tendencies and impulses a portion of the soul's potentialities is present that, under other circumstances, might just as well have made a Mirabeau[41] or Danton[42] of them. They truly harmonize with their age. In the case of Schiller, this would by no means be so hard to prove; as the poet who composed *The Robbers, Fiesko, Intrigue and Love*, he will not seem to anyone to be far removed in disposition from a Mirabeau or Danton or even a Robespierre.[43] This same soul's blood flowed likewise in Goethe, even though we might at first consider him far from being a revolutionist. But by no means is he so remote from this. There comes about in Goethe's complex nature a special complication of karmic impulses, of destiny, that places him in the world in a most unusual way, even in earliest youth.

When we trace the life of Goethe with spiritual scientific vision and disregard all other things, we find that it falls into certain periods. The first proceeds in such a way that we can

31

say that an impulse which we have already observed in his childhood continues to progress. Then something comes from without that changes the direction of his life; that is, his becoming acquainted with the Duke of Weimar in 1775. Then, again, we see how his soujourn in Rome[44] changes the course of his life, how he becomes an utterly different person through having been able to absorb this Roman life. If we should wish to view the matter more accurately, we might say that a third impulse, which comes as if from without—but this, as we shall see, would not be entirely accurate in a spiritual scientific sense—would be Goethe's friendship with Schiller[45] after he had experienced his Roman transformation.

If we study the first part of Goethe's life up to the year 1775, observing the events more intently than we usually do, we shall discover that there lives in him a powerful revolutionary mood, a rebellion against what was in his environment. His nature, however, is spread over many things. For this reason, because the impulse toward rebellion does not appear so strongly as when concentrated in Schiller's *The Robbers* but is more diffuse, it does not appear so strikingly. Anyone, however, who is able to enter in a spiritual scientific way into Goethe's boyhood and youth finds in him a spiritual force of life, brought with him through birth, that could not have been present throughout his life if certain events had not occurred. What was living within him as the Goethe individuality was far greater than what could be taken up and expressed in life by his organism.

This is obvious in Schiller. His early death was due primarily to the fact that his organism was consumed by his mighty, spiritual vitality.[46] This is obvious. Indeed, it is known that after his death his heart was found to be dried up, as it were. He sustained himself as long as possible only by his powerful spiritual vitality, but this also devoured his bodily life.

With Goethe, this force of soul became even stronger, and yet he lived to an advanced age. What enabled him to live so long? You will recall that I reminded you yesterday of a fact that intervened significantly in Goethe's life. After he had spent some years in Leipzig as a student,[47] he became seriously ill and stood face to face with death. He virtually looked death in the face. This illness is, to be sure, a natural phenomenon in the organism. However, we never learn to understand a man who creates out of the elemental forces of the world—indeed, we never learn really to understand any man—unless we take into consideration such events in the course of his karma. What really happened to Goethe when he became ill in Leipzig? We may describe it as a complete loosening of the etheric body in which the life forces of the soul had been active until then. It was loosened to such an extent that, after this illness, he no longer had that closely knit connection between the etheric and the physical bodies that he had formerly possessed.

The etheric body, however, is the supersensible member in us that really makes it possible to form concepts, to think. Abstract concepts such as we have in ordinary life, the only concepts that are approved by most persons who are materialistically disposed, come about through the fact that the etheric body is, as it were, closely united with the physical by a strong magnetic union. It is also through this fact that we possess a strong impulse to project our will into the physical world, that is, provided the astral body is strongly developed. In the case of Robespierre, Mirabeau and Danton, we have an etheric body strongly united with the physical but also a powerfully developed astral body. This works, in turn, upon the etheric body, which establishes these human individualities strongly in the physical world.

Goethe was also organized like this, but another force now worked in him and brought about a complication. The result was that the etheric body was loosened and remained so through the illness that had brought him to the point of death. When the etheric body is no longer so intimately united with the physical body, however, it no longer thrusts its forces into the physical but retains them. This explains the transformation Goethe passed through when he returned to Frankfurt. There, during his acquaintance with Fräulein von Klettenberg,[48] the mystic, and with various medical friends who were devoted to studies in alchemy, and through the writings of Swedenborg, he really developed a systematic spiritual world conception. It was still somewhat chaotic, but nevertheless a systematic spiritual world conception, and he was profoundly inclined to occupy himself with supersensible things.

These things are, however, connected with Goethe's illness. The soul that had brought this predisposition for this illness into his earthly life also brought the impulse so to prepare his etheric body through his illness that it should not be expressed merely in the physical. It maintained the urge and the capacity to become permeated with supersensible concepts. So long as we merely consider the external biographical facts of a person in a materialistic way, we never discover what subtle interrelationships exist in his stream of destiny. But, as soon as we obtain an insight into the harmony between the natural occurrences affecting his organism, such as the illness of Goethe, and what manifests itself ethically, morally, spiritually, it becomes possible for us to sense the profound effect of karma.

The revolutionary force would certainly have been manifest in Goethe in a way that would have consumed him at an early age. Since an external expression of the life of these revolutionary forces would certainly not have been possible in his environment, and since he could not have written dramas as Schiller did, this force would necessarily have consumed him. It was turned aside through the loosening of the connection of the magnetic union between his etheric and physical bodies.

Here we see how a natural event seems to enter with immense significance into the life of a human being. Undoubtedly, it points to a deeper interrelationship than the one the biographers generally wish to reveal. The significance of an illness to a man cannot be explained on the basis of hereditary tendencies but rather points to the connection between a man and the world in such a way that this relationship must be conceived spiritually. You will note also how Goethe's life was thus complicated; such experiences determine how we take things in and what we are ourselves.

Goethe now comes to Strassburg[49] with an etheric body that is in a sense filled with occult knowledge, and in this condition he meets Herder, whose vast conceptions had to become something quite different in Goethe because the same conditions did not exist in Herder's more subtle constitution. This event of near death appeared in Goethe at the end of the sixties in Leipzig, but its force had been prepared long before that. Anyone who undertakes to trace such an illness to external or merely physical events has not yet attained the same standpoint in the spiritual sphere as that occupied by the natural scientist who knows that what follows must not be viewed necessarily as the result of what it follows. This tendency to isolate himself from the world to some degree was a manifestation of the connection between physical and etheric bodies. It was always present in Goethe, and it really only became a crisis through his illness.

In anyone possessing a compact connection between the physical and etheric bodies, the external world exerts its influence and, as it makes impressions on the physical body, they pass over immediately into the etheric body; this is one and the same thing. Such a person simply lives in direct contact with the impressions of the external world. In Goethe's case, the impressions are, of course, made upon the physical body, but the etheric body does not immediately respond because it is loosened. As a result, such a person can be more isolated, in a sense, from his environment, and a more complicated process takes place when an impression is made on his physical body. If you establish a connection between this organic structure of Goethe and the fact that, as we learn from his biography, he lays himself open even to historic events without forcing them, you have then arrived at an understanding of the peculiar functioning of his nature. I told you that he took the autobiography of Gottfried of Berlichingen and, influenced only by the dramatic impulses received from Shakespeare, did not really alter much in it. So he did not call it a drama but *The History of the Iron-handed Gottfried of Berlichingen, Dramatized.* You see, this soft and almost timid handling of things, as I might call it, without taking hold of them forcefully is due to his quite unusual connection between the etheric and physical bodies.

This relationship between the etheric and physical bodies was not present in Schiller. For this reason, he creates characters that he has certainly not derived from external impressions but has formed forcefully out of his own nature; Karl Moor is an example. Goethe, however, needs the influence of life, but he does not force it; he only helps with a light touch to elevate the living into a work of art.

It was the same when he was confronted with the experiences that he later reduced to artistic form in *Werther.* His own life situations as well as those of his friend Jerusalem[50] are not twisted; he does not alter the form greatly but takes life and retouches it a little. Through the delicate manner in which he renders assistance by means of his etheric body, life is transformed into a work of art. But because of this organization he gains, I might say, only an indirect contact with life, and thereby he prepares his karma in this incarnation.

Goethe goes to Strassburg. In addition to the experience that advanced him on his way, he experienced also, as you know, the romantic involvement with Friederike, the daughter of the pastor in Sesenheim.[51] His affections were deeply involved in this relationship, and many moral doubts may be raised against the course of it—doubts that may also be fully justified. We are not now concerned with that aspect of the matter, but rather with an understanding of it. Goethe really passed through everything that, in another, not only must, but obviously would, have led to a permanent life union. But he does not experience directly. Through what I have explained, a sort of chasm had been created between his unusual inner nature and the external world. Just as he does not alter by force what is living in the external world but only delicately modifies its form, he also does not carry his feelings and sensations, which he can experience only in his etheric body, through the physical body to such a firm contact with the external world—something that, in others, would have led to quite definite events in life. So he withdraws from Friederike Brion, but one must accept this from the viewpoint of the soul.

The last time he went to Sesenheim, he met himself; you can read of this in his autobiography.[52] Goethe meets Goethe! Long afterward he related how he then encountered himself, Goethe meeting Goethe. He sees himself; he drives out to Sesenheim and Goethe comes to meet him, not in the same clothing he was wearing, however, but in another outfit. When he went there again many years later to visit his old acquaintances, he realized that he was unintentionally actually wearing the clothes in which he had seen himself many years before. We must believe this even took place in the same way we believe anything else he relates. Considering the love of truth with which he described his life to us, to find fault with it is not appropriate.

How does it happen, then, that Goethe, so remote that he could actually withdraw, and yet in such loose contact with the circumstances that for anyone else it would have led to something quite different—how does it come about that he meets himself? Now a man who has an experience in his etheric body finds that it easily takes objective form when the etheric body is loosened. He sees the experience as something external; it is projected outside him. This actually happened to Goethe. In a moment peculiarly appropriate, he saw the other Goethe, the etheric Goethe who lived in him, who remained united in karma with Friederike of Sesenheim, and he met himself as a ghost. But this is just the kind of event that so profoundly confirms what is to be perceived from the facts regarding his nature.

We see here how a man may stand within external events and how it is also necessary to grasp the special, individual way in which he stands among them. It is a complicated relationship that exists between the human being and the world; it is complicated also by the interrelationship between what he brings from the past into the present. Through the fact, however, that Goethe had wrenched his inner nature out of the corporeal connection, it was possible for him even in his early youth to cherish in his soul the profound truths that so astonish us in his *Faust*. I say *astonish* purposely for the simple reason that they really must astonish us. I scarcely know anything more simple-minded than when biographers of Goethe repeat over and over the statement, "Goethe is Faust and Faust is Goethe." I have often read this in biographies of Goethe. It is, of course, an ordinary bit of nonsense. What we really have in *Faust*, when we permit it to work on us in the right way, so impresses us that we must sometimes say that we cannot imagine that Goethe had a direct experience of a similar kind or could even know of it. Yet there it is expressed in *Faust*.

Faust constantly grows beyond Goethe. This can be understood completely by one who knows the surprise experienced by a poet when he has this composition before him. That is, we do not have to suppose that the poet must

always be as great as his work, anymore than a father must
be as great in forces of soul and genius as his son; the truly
poetic creative process is something living; just as one cannot say it is also impossible to assert that one who is spiritually creative never creates above his own level. But
through the inner state of isolation that I have described in
reference to Goethe, those profound insights in his soul appear that we find in reading his *Faust*. Such works are not
poetic compositions like others. The *Faust* poem flows from
the entire spirit of the fifth post-Atlantean culture period; it
grows far beyond Goethe. Much that we experience in connection with the world and its process of becoming sounds
forth to us from *Faust* in a strange manner. Call to mind the
passage you have just heard:[53]

> To us, my friend, the ages that are passed
> A book with seven seals, close fastened, are
> And what the spirit of the times men call
> Is merely their own spirit after all. . . .[54]

These words by Faust himself are passed over too lightly.
One who experiences the statement in its fullest depths is
reminded of much that confirms its truth. Consider the
knowledge possessed by modern man of the Greeks and the
spiritual life of Greece, through Aeschylus, Sophocles, Eu-
ripides! Suppose men steep themselves in this Greek spiritual life—let us say, in Sophocles. Is Sophocles a book with
seven seals? That will not easily be admitted! More than
eighty dramas were written by Sophocles,[55] who lived to be
ninety-one; only seven of these dramas now survive. Do we
really know a man if he has written eighty-one or more
dramas and only seven of them survive? Is this not truly a
book with seven seals? How can anyone assert that he
knows the Greek world from what has been handed down to
us, when he must simply recognize the fact that seventy-
four of Sophocles' dramas, by which the Greeks were

fascinated and inspired, are nonexistent? Many of the dramas of Aeschylus no longer exist. Poets lived in Greek times whose names are not even known any longer. Are not the times past truly a book with seven seals? We must admit this when we consider such external facts, and

> . . .'tis delightful to transport
> Oneself into the spirit of the past,
> To see in times before us how a wise man thought,
> And what a glorious height we have achieved at last.[56]

Wagner types believe they are able to transplant themselves quite easily into the spirit of a wise man; that is, when somebody before them has already done the exercise! It is a pity that we cannot put to the proof what the critics would have to write about *Hamlet* if it had been written today and were to be performed for them by some large municipal theater, or if a drama of Sophocles should be presented for them at this very moment. Perhaps no impression would be made on these gentlemen even by what Sophocles had to do to convince his relatives of his greatness in his advanced old age of ninety-one. His relatives had had to wait so long for their inheritance that they tried to prove he had become feeble-minded and could no longer manage his property. He had no other way to protect himself than by writing the *Oedipus in Colonna*, thus proving that he was not yet in his dotage. Whether this would work with present-day critics I do not know, but at that time it did help. Anyone who enters deeply into the tragedy of the ninety-one year old Sophocles, however, will be able to estimate how difficult it is to find the way to a human individuality and how such an individuality is bound up in the most complicated fashion with world events! Many things could be adduced to show under what deep layers we must penetrate in order to understand the world. But how much is alive, even in the earliest parts of *Faust*, of that wisdom that is necessary for

40

an understanding of the world! This wisdom must be attributed to the peculiar course of Goethe's destiny which reveals to us in a real sense that nature and the work of the spirit are a unity in human development and that an illness not only has an external significance but may also possess spiritual meaning.

Thus we see a decided continuation of the karmic impulses that existed in Goethe. Then in 1775, however, his connection with the Duke of Weimar appeared as if from without. Goethe is called from Frankfurt to Weimar. What does this signify in his life? To further understand the life of a man, we must first understand what such an event means to his life. I know how little inclined the present world is really to arouse those forces of the soul that are necessary to fully sense and feel such a phenomenon—to completely feel what is already alive in the first scenes of *Faust*. In order to write the *Monologue in the Study, Spirit of the Earth* that has just been presented, a richness of soul is needed, and it will cause one who beholds it to linger long in an attitude of fervent reverence. One is often pained to the depths of one's soul to realize that the world is really still decidedly dull and cannot feel what is truly *great*. But, if we feel such a thing completely, we shall then also see where one who is deeply permeated with spiritual science arrives in his feeling. Such a person comes to the point of saying to himself that something lived in Goethe that consumed him; he couldn't go on in such a way.

Two things must be clear if we are to appreciate, in the proper sense and in the right light, these first scenes of *Faust*. We might imagine that Goethe had written them gradually between his twenty-fifth and fiftieth years, in which case they would not have strained his soul so intensely, nor been such a burden. Certainly! But this is impossible because, after his thirtieth or thirty-fifth year, the youthful force necessary to give such form to these scenes would have been lacking. In accordance with his individuality, he had to write them in those early years, but to continue to live thus was no longer possible. He needed something like a damper, a partial soul-sleep, to reduce the intensity of the fire that burned in his soul as he wrote these first scenes. Then, the Duke of Weimar called him to make him a minister in Weimar. As I have already said, Goethe was a good minister, and while he labored assiduously, he could refresh himself by partially sleeping off what burned in his soul.

There is really a tremendous difference between Goethe's mood up to 1775 and that after 1775, a difference that may be compared with a mighty wakefulness followed by a subdued life. The word "Dumpfheit," an inner feeling of numbness, comes into his mind when he describes his life in Weimar, where he engages himself so much in events but responds to them more than at an earlier age, when he had rebelled against them. It is peculiar that after this dampening down for ten years there followed a period when events confronted him in a more gentle way. Just as the life of sleep is by no means a direct effect of the preceding daytime life, so also this sleep life of Goethe was not at all the result of what had gone before. The interrelationships are far greater than is generally supposed. I have already frequently pointed out that it is indicative of a superficial view when, to the question—Why does a man sleep?—the answer is given: Because he is tired. This is a lazy truth and one that is itself asleep since it is nonsense. Otherwise, it would not be true that individuals such as non-working persons living on their private incomes who are certainly not tired, fall comfortably asleep after a full meal when they are expected to listen to something that does not particularly interest them. Tired they certainly are not. The fact is not that we sleep because we are tired, but waking and sleeping are a rhythmic life process, and when it is time or necessary for us to sleep, we become weary. We are tired because we ought to sleep; we

do not sleep because we are tired. But I will not discuss this
further just now.

Just consider in what a tremendous interrelationship the
rhythm of sleeping and waking stands. It is a reproduction
within the nature of man of day and night in the cosmos. It
is natural, of course, that a materialistic science should
undertake to explain sleep as resulting from weariness caused
by the day's activities, but the reverse is true. The explanation of the rhythm of sleeping and waking must be drawn
from the cosmos, from vast interrelationships. They also explain that the period when *Faust* was fermenting in the soul
of Goethe was followed by the ten-year period of dampening
in Weimar. Here your attention is called directly to his karma, about which we cannot speak further at present.

The consciousness of the ordinary human generally lets
him wake in the morning thinking he is unchanged from
what he was when he fell asleep. In reality, such is never the
case. We are never the same upon waking as we were when
we fell asleep but, as a matter of fact, we are somewhat
richer, though unconscious of it. However, just as the trough
of a wave has followed after a crest, as it was in Goethe's
Weimar years, the awakening that follows is at a higher stage;
it must follow at a higher stage because the innermost forces
strive toward this. In Goethe also the innermost forces strive
to awaken again from the inner state of numbness in Weimar to a fullness of life in an environment that could now
really bring him what he lacked. He awakened in Italy.
With his special constitution he could not have awakened in
Weimar. In this fact, however, we can see the profound
relationship between the creative work of a real artist and
his special experience.

You see, a writer who is not an artist can produce a
drama gradually without difficulty, one page at a time; he
can do this perfectly well. The great poet cannot; he needs
to be deeply rooted in life. For this reason, Goethe could

bring the most profound truths to expression in his *Faust* in relatively early youth, truths that ranged far above the capacities of his soul, but he had to set forth a rejuvenation of Faust. Just bear in mind that Faust had to come into an entirely different mood in spite of the fact that his nature was so deeply formed. In the end, in spite of all his depth, what he had taken into his soul up to that time had brought him near to suicide. He had to be rejuvenated. A lesser individual can describe perfectly well, and even in pretty verses, how a man is rejuvenated. Goethe could not do this so simply; he first had to experience his own rejuvenation in Rome. It is for this reason that the rejuvenation scene, *The Witch's Kitchen*, was written in Rome in the Villa Borghese.[57] Goethe would not have ventured to write this scene earlier.

Now, a certain condition of consciousness, even though dulled, is associated with such a rejuvenation as Goethe experienced. In his time there was not as yet a spiritual science, so this state of consciousness could not be heightened but only subdued. Furthermore, special forces are associated with such a rejuvenation as Goethe experienced. In his time there was not as yet a spiritual science, so this state of consciousness could not be heightened but only subdued. Furthermore, special forces are associated with such a rejuvenation that are projected over into the next incarnation. Here experiences are woven together that belong to the present incarnation and also much that projects its influence into the next. When we bear this in mind, we are led to consider an especially profound and significant tendency in Goethe.

You see, if I may be permitted to interject this personal comment, I have occupied myself for a number of decades with Goethe's view of nature—I may say since 1879–80, and intensively since 1885–86. During this time, I have arrived at the view that there is something in the impulse that Goethe gave to the conception of nature, which contemporary scientists and philosophers really do not understand, that can be developed, but it will take centuries to do so. It may well be, therefore, that when Goethe returns in another incarnation it will still be possible for him to work formatively on what he could not perfect in his views of nature in this incarnation. Many things that are implicit in his view of nature have not yet even been surmised. In regard to this, I have expressed myself in my book, *Goethe's World Conception*, and in the introduction to *Goethe's Natural Scientific Writings* in Kürschner's *Nationalliteratur*. We may really say, therefore, that Goethe bears within him in his view of nature something that points toward remote horizons. It is, however, intimately related with his rebirth as this was connected with the period of life through which he was passing when he was in Rome.

You may read for yourselves how I have presented these matters, how the metamorphosis of plants and animals, the archetypal plant and animal, took form during his journey in Italy; how upon his return he tackled the problem of the theory of colors, something that is scarcely understood at all at present; how he took hold of still other things. You will then see that his living penetration into a comprehensive view of nature is intimately bound up with his rebirth. To be sure, he did relate to *Faust* what he had arrived at in the course of his own life, not, however, as a minor, but as a major poet would do this. Faust experiences the Gretchen tragedy. In the midst of it, we are suddenly faced with Faust's view of nature, which admittedly is closely related with Goethe's. It is expressed in the following words of Faust:

Exalted spirit, all you gave me, all
That I have asked. And it was not in vain
That amid flames you turned your face toward me.
You gave me royal nature as my own dominion,
Strength to experience her, enjoy her. Not

The cold amazement of a visit only
You granted me, but let me penetrate
Into her heart as into a close friend's.
You lead the hosts of all that is alive
Before my eyes, teach me to know my brothers
In quiet bushes and in air and water.
And when the storm roars in the wood and creaks,
The giant fir tree, falling, hits and smashes
The neighbor branches and the neighbor trunks,
And from its hollow thud the mountain thunders,
Then you lead me to this safe cave and show
Me to myself, and all the most profound
And secret wonders of my breast are opened.[58]

A great world conception, ascribed by Goethe to Faust! Only during the journey to Italy had Goethe acquired it with such penetration of soul. The scene beginning, "Spirit sublime, thou gavest me, gavest me all," was also written in Rome, not earlier. These two scenes—the rejuvenation scene in *The Witch's Kitchen*, and the scene, *Forest and Cave*, were the portions that were written in Rome.

Here you see a real rhythm in Goethe's life that reveals an inner impulse just as the rhythm of waking and sleeping reveals an inner impulse in the human being. In a life such as Goethe's we can study certain laws in an especially clear light, but we shall also learn that the laws we discover in great personalities may become important for the life of every individual human being. In the last analysis, the laws working in an eminent human being apply to all individuals. Tomorrow we will continue to speak of the relationships of life as they may be grasped from this point of view.

46

III

Now, I wish to approach the problem we are dealing with in these reflections from another point of departure. In spiritual science we must proceed so that we encircle the problem, in a sense, and approach it from various points and directions. When we observe a life such as Goethe's, one thing must strike us that may become a profound riddle in the evolution of humanity. This is so even when we take into consideration repeated lives on earth and include them in our deliberation of the molding of a human life. The problem is this: What is the reason that individuals such as Goethe are capable of creating something so significant out of their inner nature, as he did especially through his *Faust*, and through this exert so important an influence on the rest of humanity? How does it happen that certain individuals are separated from the rest of humanity and are summoned by cosmic destiny to do something of such significance? We compare such an important life and work with that of each individual and ask ourselves: What conclusion can be drawn from the difference between these individual lives and the lives of these preeminent persons?

This question can be answered only when we observe life somewhat more thoroughly with the tools provided by spiritual science. To begin with, all that a person can know, especially in our time, is intended to conceal and disguise certain things and to keep unprejudiced reflections out of touch with them. This often makes it necessary in the sphere of spiritual science to adapt what we say to what can be understood by others.

Now, the description we generally give in spiritual science is that man consists of physical body, etheric body, astral body, and ego. In explaining the alternation between waking and sleeping, we say that in the waking state the ego and astral body are within the physical and etheric bodies but, during sleep, the ego and astral body are outside. This is adequate for a primary understanding, and it corresponds exactly with the spiritual scientific facts. But the truth is that we give only a part of the full reality in this description. We can never encompass the full reality in just one description, and thus we exhaust only part of anything we describe. We always need to seek light from other sources in order to properly illumine the part of reality already described. Here it must be stated that, speaking generally, sleeping and waking are really a sort of cyclic movement. Strictly speaking, the ego and astral body are outside the physical and etheric bodies in sleep only in being outside the head. Because the ego and astral body in sleep are outside the physical and etheric head, they bring about a more vivid activity in the rest of the human organization. It is, indeed, during sleep, when the ego and astral body are working from without upon the human being, that everything in him that does not belong to the head but to other parts of his organization is subjected to a far stronger influence of the ego and astral body than when he is awake. It may even be said that the action that the ego and astral body bring to bear upon the head in the waking state is exerted upon the rest of the organism during sleep. We can, therefore, rightly compare the ego with the sun, which illumines our environment during the day but during the night, it not only is outside of us but lights the other side of the earth. So, likewise, is it day in the rest of our organism when it is night for our sensory perception, which is primarily connected with the head; reciprocally, it is night for the rest of our organism when it is day for our head; that is, the rest of our organism is more or less withdrawn from the ego and astral body when we are awake. If we wish to understand the entire human being, this is something that must also be added to illumine the full reality.

Now, it is important to grasp correctly the connection of the psychic with the physical in man if we wish to understand properly what I have just told you. I have often stressed the fact that the nervous system of the physical organism is a unified organization, and it is really sheer nonsense, impossible to prove anatomically, to classify the nerves as sensory and motor. They are organized as a unity and all have *one* function. The so-called motor nerves are distinguished from the so-called sensory only to the extent that the sensory nerves are arranged to serve our perception of the outer world whereas the motor nerves serve for the perception of our organism. It is not the function of a motor nerve to cause my hand to move, for example; this is sheer nonsense. It exists for the purpose of perceiving my hand's movement from within. The sensory nerves, however, serve in the perception of the outer world. This is their sole distinction. As you know, our nervous system is divided into three branches: those nerves whose main center is the brain, centered in the head, the nerves that are centered in the spinal cord, and the nerves that belong to the ganglionic system [autonomic nervous system]. These are, in essence, the three kinds of nerves, and the important point is to know how they are related to the spiritual members of our organism.

Which is the finest and most advanced member of the nervous system and which the least? Quite obviously, those who adhere to the ordinary scientific world conception will answer that the nervous system of the brain is naturally the noblest because it distinguishes man from the animal. But such is not the case. This nervous system of the brain is really connected with the entire organization of the etheric body. Obviously, additional relationships exist everywhere so that our brain system is naturally related to the astral body or the ego. But these are secondary relationships. Those between our nervous system of the brain and our etheric body are the primary, original ones. This has nothing to do with the view I once presented in which I explained that the entire nervous system has been brought into existence with the help of the astral body. This is something quite different and must be kept quite distinct. In its original potentiality, the nervous system was brought into existence during the Moon period. It has evolved further, however, and other relationships have been introduced since its first formation, so that our brain system really has its most intimate and important relationship with our etheric body. The spinal cord system has its most intimate and primary relationships with our present astral body, and the ganglionic system is related with the actual ego. These are the primary relationships as they now exist.

Considering all this, we shall readily see that an especially active relationship exists during the state of sleep between our ego and ganglionic system, which extends throughout the trunk of the body, ensheathing the spinal cord, etc. But these relationships are lessened during the waking life of day. They are more intimate during sleep, as are the relationships between the astral body and spinal cord nerves. We may say, then, that during sleep especially intimate relationships obtain between our astral body and the nerves of the spinal cord, and between our ego and ganglionic system. To a greater or lesser degree, we live during sleep, as regards our ego, in a strong connection with our ganglionic system. Someday, through a thorough study of the puzzling world of dreams, people will come to know what I am here pointing out on the basis of spiritual scientific investigation.

Taking this into consideration, you will arrive at a transition to another essential, important thought. Something significant for our life must be due to the rhythmical alternation that occurs in the living union between the ego and the ganglionic system, and between the astral body and the spinal cord system. This rhythmical alternation is identical with the alternation of sleeping and waking. Thus, you will not be surprised when the statement is made that, just because the ego is really so truly in the ganglionic system and the astral body is so truly in the spinal cord system, man wakes in relation to the ganglionic and spinal cord systems during sleep, and sleeps in this relationship while awake. Here we can only ask how it comes about that so little is known of that vivid state of waking that must really be developed during sleep. Well, when you consider how man has come to be, that his ego has taken its place in him only during earthly existence and is, therefore, really the baby among his human members, it will not then seem amazing that this ego life cannot yet bring to consciousness what it experiences in the ganglionic system during sleep, whereas it can bring into full consciousness what it experiences when it is in the head, which is primarily the result of all those impulses that were at work during the Moon, Sun, etc., periods.

What the ego can bring to consciousness depends on the instrument it can use. That used during the night is still comparatively delicate. As I have pointed out in previous lectures, the rest of the organism really developed later than the head, has only been added later, and is an appendage of the fully developed head organism. When we say that relative to his physical body, man has passed through longer or shorter stages beginning with Saturn, we are referring only to his head. What is attached to his head is in many ways a later formation of the Moon period, and even of the earth. It is for this reason that the vivid life that is developed during sleep, and that has its organic seat to a large extent in the spinal cord and ganglionic systems, enters consciousness at first only in a small degree. But it is not because of this a less significantly vivid life. One can say with equal justification that during sleep the possibility is offered to man to descend into his ganglionic system and that in the waking state the possibility is given to ascend to his senses and brain system. You will surely say, "How this complicates and confuses everything that we have acquired!" Man, however, is a complicated being and we do not learn to understand him when we fail to permit these complex complications to work upon us.

Now just suppose that what I have described regarding Goethe actually happens to someone and his etheric body is loosened. Then an entirely different relationship comes about during the waking life between his soul-spiritual and his organic-physical nature. As I expressed it yesterday, he is put on a sort of isolated pedestal. But such an effect can never come about without being followed by another. It is important to bear in mind that such a relationship does not occur one-sidedly, but brings about another. If one expresses what I characterized yesterday somewhat more crudely, we may even say that the loosening of the etheric body influences the entire waking life in a certain way, but this cannot happen without also influencing the sleeping life. The result is simply that the person comes into looser relationships with his brain impressions. Because of this, he enters into more intimate relationships during the waking state with his spinal cord nerves and ganglionic system. At the time that Goethe fell ill, he developed, as it were, a looser relationship with his brain but at the same time he experienced a more intimate relationship with his ganglionic and spinal cord systems.

What is actually happening as a result of this experience? What does it mean to say that a more intimate relationship comes about with the ganglionic and spinal cord systems? It means that the individual enters into an entirely different relationship with the external world. We are, of course, always in the most intimate relationship with the outer world, but we merely fail to observe how intimate the relationship is. But I have often called your attention to the fact that the air that you hold within you at one moment is, in the next, outside, and then different air is taken in. Thus, what is outside takes on the form of the body and unites with it when you inhale. It is only seemingly true that the organism is distinct from the external world. It is a member of it and belongs to it. If, therefore, such a modification in an individual's relationship to the external world occurs as has been described, it makes itself felt strongly in his life. Indeed, it may be said that in such a personality as Goethe's, the lower nature, which we generally connect with the spinal cord and ganglionic systems, must come to the fore all the more strongly through this process. As the forces draw back from the head, the ganglionic and spinal cord systems take possession of them in larger measure.

An understanding for what really happens here is acquired only when we permeate ourselves with the knowledge that what we call the intellect and reason is not really so closely bound up with our individuality as is ordinarily assumed. It is clear that contemporary basic conceptions of these things are completely wrong; in part, it is in these matters that contemporary views are least frequently right. This has been especially evident in the muddle-headed behavior by some people in our age, including members of the most learned circles, when they tried to interpret their experiences with so-called dogs, apes, horses, etc. As you know, reports came out of the blue and were circulated about educated horses that can speak and do all sorts of things, about a highly educated dog that made a great stir in Mannheim, and an educated monkey in the Frankfurt zoo that had been taught to do arithmetic, as well as other things that one cannot mention in polite society. The Frankfurt chimpanzee, in other words, has been trained in certain natural necessities to behave like humans rather than monkeys. I will not pursue this further, but all this caused the greatest astonishment, not only among laymen, but also among professionals. They were actually enraptured, especially when the Mannheim dog, after one of its beloved offspring died, wrote a letter telling how this dear puppy would be together with the archetypal soul, what it would be like and so on. That dog wrote a most intelligent letter.

Well, we need not elaborate on these specially complicated expressions of intelligence, but what stands out is that all these various animals performed feats of arithmetic. A great deal of attention was then given to the investigation of what such animals can achieve. Something quite unusual came to light in the case of the Frankfurt ape. It was possible to witness that when he was given a problem in addition to which he had to find a definite answer he pointed to the correct number in a series placed side by side. It was then discovered that this educated ape had simply formed the habit of being guided by the direction of the glance of his trainer. Then some of those who had previously been astonished said, "He has no trace of a mind; his training is everything!" In other words, the animal was taking his direction from his trainer and followed nothing more than a somewhat complicated training procedure. Just as a dog fetches a stone when it is thrown, so did the ape produce from the series of numbers the one indicated by the glance of his trainer.

Upon more thorough investigation, similar findings will undoubtedly be obtained in experiments with the other animals. Whatever, we cannot suppress our astonishment that people are so amazed when animals perform something that is seemingly human. How much more objective understanding, how much intellect, is actually associated with the so-called instinctual behavior in animals. As a matter of fact, the enormously important achievements and profoundly significant connections in the animal realm cause us to admire the wisdom underlying all happenings. We do not have wisdom merely in our heads; wisdom surrounds us everywhere like light, working everywhere, even through the animal kingdom. In the presence of such unusual phenomena as we have mentioned, only those people are astonished who have not seriously dealt with scientific developments. To all those who today are writing such learned tracts on the Mannheim dog and other dogs, on horses and the Frankfurt ape, along with much else because these are not unique—to all these I should like to read a passage from *Comparative Psychology* by Carus[59] that was published as early as 1866. Since they are not here, I will read the passage to you. Carus writes:

> . . . When, therefore, the dog, for example, has long been treated with kindness and affection by his master, the human traits imprint themselves upon the animal quite objectively, even though it has no conception of goodness as such; they blend with the sensory image of this person that the dog has often seen and cause the animal to recognize him, even apart from the sense of sight, merely through scent or hearing, as the one from whom something good once came to him. If, therefore, some suffering befalls this man, if he is even deprived, perhaps, of the possibility of continuing his kindness to the dog, the animal feels this as something evil inflicted upon him and is moved thereby to rage and revenge; all this occurs without any abstract thinking whatever, but only through the succession of one sensory image after another.

It is certainly true that for the dog sensory image follows sensory image; however, intelligence and wisdom are at the bottom of the phenomenon per se. Carus continues as follows:

> Yet is it strange how closely *actual thinking is approached* and may be resembled in its results by such a peculiar

weaving together, separating and again joining together of the images of the inner sense. Thus, I once saw a well-trained white poodle (this was not the Mannheim dog because this book was written in 1866) that correctly picked out and placed together letters for words spoken to him. He also *seemed* to solve simple problems in arithmetic by bringing together figures written, as were the letters, on separate sheets of paper, *seemed* to be able to count how many ladies were present in the company, and did other similar things. Of course, if all this had depended upon a *real understanding of number* as a mathematical concept, it would not have been possible without actual *reflection*. It turned out, however, that the dog had simply been trained to pick up, on a slight gesture or sound from his master, the paper bearing the required letter or number from the series of sheets laid before him. Upon another indication through an equally slight sound, like the clicking of the thumbnail against the nail of another finger, he would lay the sheet down in another row, thus performing what seemed to be a miracle.[60]

You see, not only the phenomenon, but also its explanation has long been known. Only now has this explanation been furnished again by the scientists because people pay no attention to what has been accomplished in the past. It is only for this reason that such things occur, and they bear testimony, not to our advanced science, but to our advanced ignorance!

On the other hand, certain objections have rightly been raised. If we had only these explanations (as we have heard them today) they might be considered equally naive, because Hermann Bahr[61] has quite correctly reminded us of the following. Herr Pfungst[62] demonstrated that the horses reacted to extremely slight cues made unconsciously and unperceived by their trainers. But Herr Pfungst was able to perceive these exceedingly slight gestures only after he had worked for a long time in his physiological laboratory constructing an apparatus to detect them. Bahr justifiably raises the objection that it was certainly most peculiar that only the horse should be clever enough to observe the gestures, whereas a university instructor had to work for years constructing an apparatus to do so—I believe it took him ten or more years. In all such things there is obviously a bit of truth, but we must simply view them in the right way.

With the proper perception, one can obviously explain such phenomena only when one thinks of objective wisdom and understanding as qualities that, along with instinctive behavior, have been instilled in things, and when one thinks of an animal as part of a complete system of interrelated objective wisdom permeating the world. In other words, they can be explained only when we are no longer limited to the idea that wisdom has come into the world through man alone, but recognize that wisdom is to be found throughout the universe. Man, by reason of his special organization, is able to perceive more of this wisdom than other beings, and is thus distinguished from them. Because of his organization, he can perceive more than they, but through the wisdom implanted in them, they can perform wisdom-filled tasks as he can. It is, however, a different kind of wisdom. The phenomena of these unusual expressions of wisdoms are really far less important to serious observers of the world than the phenomena that are always spread out before their eyes. These are far more important and, if you take this into consideration, you will no longer find incomprehensible what I am about to say.

An animal, far more intensely than man, fits into the universal wisdom and is quite intimately united with it. Its orders, so to speak, are far more compulsory than those of

man. Human beings are much freer, and so it is possible for
them to reserve forces for the cognition of interrelationships. The essential point is that the physical body of an
animal—especially the higher ones—is fitted into the same
universal interrelationships as man's etheric body. Thus,
man *knows* more of the cosmic relationships, but animals
are far more intimately united with them; they are far closer
to, and more interwoven with, them. Therefore, if you take
this objectively dominant reason into consideration tell
yourself this: "We are surrounded not only by air and light
but also by governing reason; we do not move merely
through illumined space but also through the space of wisdom and governing reason." You will then fully understand
what it means for a person to be fitted into the world in
regard to the finer relationships of his or her organs, and not
just in an ordinary way. In normal life, a man, for example,
is joined to spiritual cosmic relationship in such a fashion
that the connection between his ego and ganglionic system,
and between his astral body and spinal cord system, are
greatly impaired during the waking life of day. But because
these connections are subdued, he is not too attentive in ordinary, normal life to what is going on around him. It would
be possible for him to observe this only if he really should
see with his ganglionic system as he otherwise perceives
with his head.

If, however, as in the special case of Goethe, the astral
body is brought into a more vivid relationship with the
spinal cord system and the ego with the ganglionic, because
the ether body has withdrawn from the head, then far more
vivid intercourse occurs with what is going on in our sur-
roundings. But it is concealed from us in normal life
because it is only while we are asleep at night that we enter
into relationship with our spiritual environment. Here you
arrive at an understanding of how the things Goethe has
written were for him genuine perceptions, and although

these could naturally not have been so clear as our sensory perceptions of the external world, yet they are clearer than the perceptions that an ordinary man has of his spiritual environment. Now, what did Goethe perceive in this way with special vividness? Let us grasp this point clearly through a special instance.

Through the complications of his particular karma, Goethe was destined to enter a life of scholarship and knowledge differently from an ordinary scholar. What did he experience through this? You see, for many centuries it has been so that a man who grows into intimate union with a life of learning has experienced a significant discord. To be sure, today it is more concealed than in Goethe's time, but it nevertheless is experienced because there is an enormous field in science that has been preserved from the fourth post-Atlantean epoch in the terminologies and systems of words that we are compelled to acquire. We trade more than we realize in words. All this has been obscured somewhat through the experimentation that has gradually been introduced since the nineteenth century, and a person now grows into his knowledge so that he sees more than he did earlier. Such sciences as jurisprudence, for instance, have descended somewhat from the specially lofty positions they previously occupied. But when jurisprudence and theology still occupied their specially lofty stations, the areas of learning man was trying to penetrate were really comprehensive systems of words, and the same is true of other things that had to be taken in as an inheritance from the fourth post-Atlantean period.

Along with this, what arises from the needs of the fifth post-Atlantean period made itself felt in an ever increasing way; that is, the life that arises from the great achievements of the new period. This is not realized by anyone who is simply driven from one lecture to another, but Goethe experienced it most intensely. I say that a person who is simply driven from one lecture to another does not sense it, but he passes through it nonetheless. He really passes through it. Here we touch the edge of a certain mystery of modern life. We can judge students who are enrolled in courses according to what they experience and what they are conscious of. But what they experience is not the whole story. Their inner nature is something quite different. If these individuals who are experiencing these overlapping layers of the fourth and fifth post-Atlantean epochs really knew what a certain part of their being is going through unconsciously, they would then have an entirely different understanding of what Goethe, even in youth, concealed mysteriously in his *Faust*. Countless persons who are finding their way into contemporary education are unconsciously sharing in this experience.

We must, therefore, remind ourselves that, by reason of all that Goethe had acquired because of his special karma, those with whom he came into close relationship during his youth were quite different to him than they would have been if he had not had this special karma. He sensed and felt how the people with whom he became intimately associated had to stupefy the Faustian life within them so that they no longer possessed it. He was able to sense this because what lived mysteriously in his fellow men made an impression on him such as is made by one person on another only when an especially intimate relationship, indeed when love, develops between them. In such a case of ordinary life, the connection of the ego with the ganglionic system, and of the astral body with the spinal cord system is highly active, although this is not consciously perceived as such. Something very special is activated. But what is otherwise active only in a love relationship came about in Goethe vis à vis a far larger number of people, so that he experienced a tremendous, more or less subconscious, compassion for the poor fellows—excuse the expression—who did not know what their inner natures were going through as they were driven from class to class and from examination to examination. This was felt by him and it gave him a rich experience.

Experiences become conceptions. Ordinary experiences become the conceptions of everyday life, but these particular experiences become the conceptions, the mental images, that Goethe poured tumultously into *Faust*. They were nothing but actual experiences that he gained from the most extensive environment because his ganglionic and spinal cord life was stimulated to more than normal wakefulness. This was the opposite from the subdued head life, but it was a potentiality in him even in his boyhood. We can see this from his description of what became active in him: not only what ordinarily engages people, say in piano lessons,[63] became active in him but also the entire being. Goethe partook much more in the happenings of real life as a whole person than others, and we must say, therefore, that he was more wide-awake during the day than they. During the time in his youth when he was working on *Faust*, he was more awake during the day, and because of this he also needed what I described yesterday as the time of sleep—the ten years in Weimar. This dampening was necessary.

This, however, is just what happens to a greater or lesser degree in every human being during the course of life, only in Goethe it took place more intensely. He was simply drawn somewhat more consciously than other men into the surrounding wisdom-filled and purely spiritual influences. He became aware of what lives and weaves mysteriously within men. What, then, is this really? When we are put into the world in our ordinary and brutal waking life together with our ego, we are bound up with the world through our senses and our ordinary perceptions. But you will agree that we are now much more closely bound with this world. Our ego is, indeed, in an especially intimate relation with our ganglionic system, and the astral body with the spinal cord system. Through this relationship, we have really a far more comprehensive connection with our environing world than through the sensory system of our head.

Now you must bear in mind that man needs the rhythmic alternation of his ego and astral body in his head during the waking life of day, and outside his head during sleep; because they are outside his head during sleep, they develop an inner active life in connection with the other systems, as I have indicated. The ego and the astral body need this alternation of sinking downward into the head and rising out of it. When man's ego and astral body are outside his head, he not only develops that intimate relationship with the rest of his organism through the ganglionic and spinal cord systems, but he also develops spiritual relationships with the spiritual world. Thus, we may say that an especially active, vivid connection with the spinal cord and ganglionic systems corresponds to an active psychic-spiritual life with the spiritual world. Since we are obliged to assume that the soul-spiritual is outside the head at night, and since this causes the development of an especially active life in the rest of the organism, we must then say that during the life of day, when the ego and the astral body are more within the head, we are in turn experiencing a spiritual symbiosis with the surrounding spiritual world. In a certain sense, we submerge ourselves in an inner spiritual world in sleep, but in a surrounding spiritual world when we awake.

This state of being one with the surrounding spiritual world is more pronounced in Goethe. He is, as it were, dreaming during a state of wakefulness—just as the ordinary person does not always fall into a deep, dreamless sleep. It is seldom that anyone dreams consciously in this way during the life of the day, but people like Goethe pass into a state of dreaming even during the waking life. The forces that remain unconscious in other people become, in a certain sense, dream-forms of life for people like Goethe.

We now have an even more exact description which

62

might tempt you to entertain the arrogant notion that all of you could easily write a *Faust* poem since you are experiencing the *Faust* dilemma by ranging out into and by living in union with the surrounding world during your daytime life. The latter is indeed true. We do experience *Faust*, but only as the opposite pole is experienced in the night through the ego and astral body when we do not dream. But since Goethe not only experienced this unconsciously, but also dreamed it, he could express it in *Faust*. He dreamed this experience and in people such as Goethe the following takes place: what they create stands in the same relationship to what the rest of us experience unconsciously as does the dream to deep sleep on the other side of our lives. This is an actual reality; the creation of the great spirits are related to the unconscious creations of other men as dream to dreamless sleep.

Even so, much remains obscure. But bear in mind that you are thereby gaining a glimpse into something that is intimately connected with human life; it may be described somewhat as follows. We could really say quite a bit about the connection between our being and the surrounding world if we could awake just to the stage of dreaming. If we were able to awaken only to the stage of dreaming, we would experience tremendous things and would also be able to describe them. But this would have a grave consequence. Just think, if all men, to express it trivially, were so conscious that they could describe everything in their environment, if they would really describe experiences, for example, like those of Goethe's as set forth in his *Faust*, what would we come to? What would the world then come to? Strange as it may seem but so it is, the world would come to a stop and would make no further progress! The moment everyone were to dream the way Goethe dreamt *Faust*, which is an utterly different kind of dreaming—the moment everyone were to dream his connection with the external world, then such people would devote all the forces developed in their inner being to such an activity. They would pour them into such things and human existence would, in some sense, consume itself. You can form a faint idea of what would happen if you just look at the many ruinous effects that are taking place because many people, although not really dreaming, imagine that they are and babble or scribble reminiscences they have picked up elsewhere. This is associated with the fact that there are entirely too many poets. Where is there anyone today who does not believe he is a poet or painter or something! The world could not continue if this were so because all good things have also their dark side, truly their dark side.

Schiller was also an important poet who dreamed much in the way I have described. Just imagine, however, that all those who in their youth were trained like Schiller to become doctors had given up the practice of medicine as he did and later, thanks to an extensive patronage, had been appointed "professor of history" without any real preparation or serious study of history! As a matter of fact, Schiller did deliver interesting lectures at the University of Jena, but his students did not get from them what they needed to learn. He also gradually stopped giving these university lectures and was happy when he did not have to give them anymore. Imagine that things would be the same with every professor of history or every young physician! Obviously, everything that is good also has its dark side. The world must be protected, so to speak, from standing still. It seems trivial to say this, but it is nevertheless a profound mystery-truth: not all people can dream in this way. The forces with which they dream must first be applied in the external world to something different so that through it a foundation may be created for a further evolution of the earth. It would come to a standstill were all men to dream as I have indicated.

Now we have reached a point where an especially paradoxical fact comes to light. To what in the world are the aforementioned forces really applied? If we observe their application in a spiritual way, they are ultimately applied to deep sleep even though you may like them to be applied to dreams. More concretely, they are applied to all that is spread out over human evolution in the most varied kinds of vocational work.

Vocational work is related to the work that was done in creating *Faust*, or in Schiller's *Wallenstein*, as deep sleep is related to dreaming. But to say that we sleep during our vocational work will seem extraordinary to you, and you will say that here, in this, you are wide awake. The truth is that there is a grand illusion in this idea that one is awake during this kind of work because what really comes into being through vocational work is not something we do in full waking consciousness. Of course, some of the effects a person's profession has upon his or her soul do enter one's consciousness, but such a person really knows nothing whatever of all that is actually present in the web of vocational labor that men are continually spinning around the world.

It is, indeed, surprising how these things are connected. Hans Sachs[64] was a shoemaker and also a poet. Jakob Boehme[65] was a shoemaker and a mystical philosopher. There you have sleeping and waking alternating through a special constellation that we may also discuss. It is possible to pass from one state into another.

What, then, is the significance of this interplay and alternation of life between vocational labor for such a man as Jakob Boehme—he really did make shoes for the good people of Görlitz—and his mystical-philosophical compositions? Many people have strange opinions of these things. Allow me to review the experience we once had when we were in Görlitz.

One evening before a lecture I was to give on Boehme,[66] I got into a conversation with a high school teacher, in which we spoke about Boehme's statue that we had just seen in the park. The people of Görlitz, as we were often told, called his monument, the "park cobbler." We remarked that it was most beautiful, but the school teacher said he did not think so. He thought it really looked like Shakespeare and one would not know from it that Boehme had been a shoemaker. He said that to represent Boehme it would have to show that he was a shoemaker. Well, one can disregard such an attitude. As Jakob Boehme was writing his great mystical-philosophical views, he was working from the results that could have come about only through the human being having evolved through the Saturn, Sun, Moon, and Earth times; that is, through the fact that a broad stream flows through these ages and finally comes to expression in these effects. This stream manifests itself in such a personality only in a way that is the result of special karmic relationships. But just as all that has traversed the Sun and Moon periods is necessary to every individual on earth, so it is also necessary, but in a special way, in order to bring out what was in Boehme.

But then, Jakob Boehme also made shoes for the worthy Görlitzers. How does all this hang together? To be sure, the fact that a man has been able to develop the skill of a shoemaker is also connected with this stream. But when the shoes are finished, they are separated from him and their function has then nothing more to do with skill but with protecting and warming feet. They go their own way in performing their functions and are separated completely from the one who makes them; what they bring about has its effects only later. In other words, this is only a beginning.

If the initial influence leading to the mystical-philosophical activity of Jakob Boehme were represented graphically, I should have to indicate the first potential toward shoemaking here at this point. This then flows on further and in the future Vulcan evolution will have developed a degree of perfection that has been reached already by what had flowed into his mystical-philosophical activity from the Saturn evolution. This is, in a sense, an end; his shoemaking is a beginning. We say, of course, that the earth is earth at present, but if we could trace things from Saturn still further back, we might then say that, relative to certain things, the earth is already Vulcan. We should then assume Saturn at this point.

Saturn   Sun   Moon   Earth

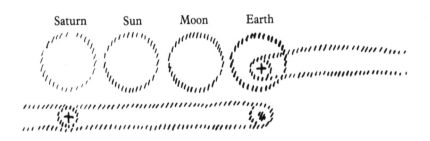

We can thus take everything in a relative way. We may say that the earth is Saturn, and that Vulcan is, in a sense, earth. What happens on the earth in the vocational labor of a man like Jakob Boehme—not in his free creative work, but what he does as vocational labor—is the beginning of something that will be as far advanced on Vulcan as the happenings on Saturn are already advanced on the earth. For Boehme to write his mystical-philosophical books on earth, it was necessary for something to have happened on Saturn that was similar to what he has done on earth in making shoes. Likewise, Boehme's shoemaking here on earth has the effect that something may be done on Vulcan that will be similar to his writing mystical philosophy here on earth.

There is something extraordinary in all this. Here is an indication of how what is often given little value on earth is so little esteemed because it is the beginning of something that will be prized in the future. In their being, human beings are, of course, much more intimately bound up with the past since they must first familiarize themselves with what is a beginning. Therefore, they often care much less for something that is a beginning than for something that has come over to them from the past. From the scope of what we are yet to be involved in during the earth period, and so that something special may then come about when the earth shall have developed further through Jupiter and Venus to Vulcan—from all this a full consciousness will develop such as the one that exists for the philosophy of Jakob Boehme on the earth. It is for this reason that the real meaning of human external labor is enveloped now in unconsciousness, just as man was shrouded in unconsciousness on Saturn; sleep consciousness was developed on the Sun, dream consciousness on the Moon, and the present condition of waking consciousness on the earth.

The human being is thus really living in a profound sleep consciousness in his involvement with everything of his vocation. Through his vocation he is really creating, not through what gives him pleasure in it, but through what is developing without his being able to enter into it; thus does he really create future values. When a person makes a nail over and over again, it certainly does not give him or her any special pleasure. But the nail becomes detached from its producer; it has quite definite tasks. As to what then happens by means of this nail is not of further concern to the worker; he does not follow up every nail he has made. But what is enveloped there in his unconscious, profoundest sleep is destined to come to life again in the future.

We have thus been able to juxtapose what the ordinary person accomplishes: first the most insignificant work in a profession and then that which appears as the highest achievement. Superior achievements are an end; the most insignificant work is always a beginning.

I wanted to place these two concepts side by side because we cannot reflect upon how the human being is bound through his karma with his vocation until we first know how his labor, which is often connected quite externally with him, is related to the entire evolution of which he is a part. We will soon develop the real question of karma as it relates to vocation. But I had first to introduce these matters so we might attain a universal concept of what flows from a human being into his or her vocation.

These things are also exceedingly useful in forming our moral sentiments in the right way. Our judgments are incorrect because we do not focus our attention on things in the right way. A seed often appears quite insignificant beside the beautiful flower of the future. Using human work as a case in point, I wanted to show you today how seed and flower are bound up in the evolution of mankind.

IV

Someone might say that the spiritual scientific reflections touching on the problem of vocation are among the least interesting. But such is not the case. This must be recognized, especially in our fifth post-Atlantean period, because in this period all human relationships will be essentially modified in comparison with those that prevailed in earlier periods of the earth. They will be so modified that man must, out of his own freedom, bring more with him than in earlier ages when his mission in the evolution of earth could be carried out almost instinctively; that is, when he received by inspiration the direction into which he had to go.

When we look back, for example, to the Egypto-Chaldean culture or to other cultures of earlier times, we shall find that the measure of freedom now given to man toward forging his external destiny—and this freedom will constantly increase—was not given him in earlier times. During the Egypto-Chaldean period, the fact that each person belonged to a certain class into which he or she was forced similar to the way an animal is forced into its species, though not so irrevocably, removed from the sphere of man's freedom much that at present belongs there. To be sure, there was a compensation for this limitation of freedom. Students of the external history of culture who are generally quite short-sighted in their thinking, usually assume that conditions in ancient times were such that those who were then guiding human affairs did so with the same impulses as the leading personalities today. But you must bear in mind that there were quite definite processes in the mysteries in ancient times whereby the guiding personalities acquainted themselves with what was willed by beings who guide life from regions outside the earth. I have told you that at certain times—we do not need now to review them—sacrificial priests carried out specified mystery rituals. As a result, certain personalities in the temples who were suited for such purposes were brought into contact with the universe, the cosmos, the extraterrestrial relationships. The consciousness of these specially qualified personalities was then inspired by beings who guided the earth from extraterrestrial regions, and what was learned from these beings determined the course of action.

I will show you through a hypothetical case how things took their course in earlier times. Suppose that today the Christmas festival was not more or less an external holiday for most people, but that in its form and time of occurrence men knew that our earth is especially fitted to receive ideas into its aura that cannot enter, for example, in summer. I have explained how the earth is awake during the winter and that Christmas time is one of the most brilliant points of this waking state. At that time the aura of the earth is permeated, interwoven, with thoughts. We may say that the earth is permeated, interwoven, with thoughts. We may say that the earth ponders the outer universe, just as we men, while in the waking state of day, reflect in our thought on what is around us. In summer the earth sleeps, so it is not possible then to find certain thoughts in it. In winter the earth is awake, and most wide awake at Christmas; then the earth's aura is interpenetrated with thoughts, and it is possible to read the will of the cosmos for our earthly events from them.

Now the sacrificial priests educated some individuals in such a way that they became sensitive and receptive to what was alive in the earth's aura. By putting these individuals into contact with the earthly thoughts that gave expression

71

to the cosmic will, the sacrificial priests in the temples could learn it from them. What they learned was to them, in a sense, the will of heaven, and from this they were able to determine who should remain in a particularly worthy position and who should be taken into the mysteries in order that he might assume a leading position in ancient government or priestly life. Humanity has now outgrown such things and is exposed to chaos in this respect; we must simply recognize this fact. The transition from the ancient, quite definite conditions in which men learned from the will of the gods what was to happen here on earth has already occurred. During the fourth post-Atlantean period, in which the individual freed himself from the will of the cosmos, these ancient customs passed over into our present more chaotic conditions. Everything tends to be handed over more completely to man. Thus, it is all the more necessary that the will of the cosmos shall penetrate earthly conditions in another way.

It would require much time to make clear how in the third Egypto-Babylonian culture period something still lived and wove in earthly life from the various vocations of men—to use a term adapted to our present conditions—that was in large measure a reproduction of the will of the cosmos. This came about as described and was disappearing during the fourth post-Atlantean period. It has vanished completely in our fifth post-Atlantean period which began, as we know, approximately in the fifteenth century. If men would pay more attention today to what is happening and stop offering a *fable convenue* in place of history, they would be able to recognize, even from external conditions, how man's relation to his vocation has changed since the fourteenth and fifteenth centuries. They would recognize from present conditions how everything will increasingly become different in the future. But a sort of anarchy would inevitably overtake mankind if no one were to grasp these deeper connections and impart to the intellectual community ideas that take into account the modifications produced by the natural course of evolution. What it has been possible to establish even from external history regarding the emergence of what we might call the modern vocational life since the fifteenth century would cause astonishment to those who are at all able to observe human life. If they would submit to the influence of all that it is possible to recognize, they would find fault with themselves, in a way, for living in such a somnolent state and for having no conception of what is connected with evolving human destiny.

Last time, I called your attention to the fact that what constitutes real vocational life is by no means so insignificant for the cosmic complex as it may at first appear. I pointed out that, as men, we have gone successively through the Saturn evolution, where the first potentialities of the physical body were prepared; the Sun period, in which the etheric man was prepared; the Moon period, in which the astral man was prepared, and that we are now passing through the earth period in which the ego develops. But other periods are to follow: The Jupiter, Venus, and Vulcan times. We may say that the earth is, in a way, the fourth stage of Saturn; likewise, Vulcan is the fourth stage of the earth. The earth is, in a sense, the Saturn of Vulcan. Just as on ancient Saturn processes occurred so intimately bound up with evolution that we owe the first potentiality of our physical body to them, which still continues to work in us, so must something happen on earth that will continue to work on in our evolution. On Vulcan it will attain a fourth stage of development, just as certain processes on Saturn have reached a fourth stage of development of earth. I pointed out that those processes that would correspond to Vulcan correspond to what we have on earth from the Saturn evolution; they represent, therefore, what works and lives in the various vocations that men take up on earth. As

73

humans pursue vocational lives, something develops on earth within their vocational activity that will be the first potentiality for Vulcan, just as the Saturn activity was the first potentiality for our physical body.

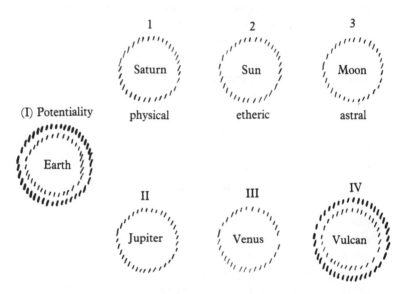

If you add to this reflection the fact that vocational life has undergone a tremendous transformation since the beginning of the fifth post-Atlantean period, you will understand how increasingly important it will become to conceive of it as a component of the entire world evolution provided you do this by means of those points of view that may be developed through spiritual science. Only by learning first to recognize the objective aspects of vocational life can we form suitable concepts regarding the karma of vocation. Of even greater interest will be the question where vocational life is going and what it will develop into from our age onward because from this we shall derive more clear-cut concepts than from today's conditions.

As can easily be recognized when we take a common sense look out into the world today, the future evolution of vocational life will consist in the ever increasing differentiation and specialization of vocations. It is not too intelligent for people to criticize the fact that, in recent times, vocations have become more specialized and that not so many centuries ago a person could find in his vocation the connections between what he was producing and what this meant for the world. He thereby would take an interest in the forming and shaping of his product because he saw clearly what his product became in life. In our times, this is no longer the case for much of humanity.

To take a radical example, a man is placed by his destiny in a factory where he perhaps makes, not a whole nail, but only part of one; this piece is then joined with another part by another man. Thus, the man who makes only part of the nail can develop no interest in how what he produced from morning until night takes its place in the relationships of life. If we compare the earlier handicraft life with the factory life of today, we are immediately aware of a radical difference between what is contemporary and what existed not too long ago. What has already come to pass in the various branches of human activity will continue to develop, and more specialization and differentiation of vocational life will necessarily occur. It is by no means especially intelligent for people to criticize this because it is a necessity in evolution; it simply will happen, and will happen more and more.

What sort of outlook is opened to us by this fact? Fundamentally, it is that men must increasingly lose interest, as we can readily imagine, in the work that occupies the greater part of their lives; in a way, they must surrender like automatons to their work in the world. But the most essential point is something else. Man's inner nature must obviously acquire the color of his outer work. Anyone who observes the historic development of humanity will certainly discover to what a large extent the men of the recent fifth post-Atlantean period have become reproductions of their vocations and how their vocational lives influence their soul lives, specializing them. This does not apply to the majority of those who live today within our Anthroposophical Society, however. They are often in the fortunate position of having detached themselves from the interconnections of life. In the fortunate position? I might just as well say in the unfortunate position! This is good fortune often only for subjective egoistic feeling. For the world, it is often bad fortune because the world will demand increasingly of men that they excel in special fields and become specialists.

But what must happen in addition to this? Their specialization will be a necessary by-product of world evolution, and this question will soon become one of the weightiest of family problems; anyone who wishes to educate children will have to understand it. To place oneself rationally within the course of evolution then will depend altogether upon an understanding of the question: How shall I place my child into the evolution of humanity? What is still possible in many cases today, even though it is only a residue left over from ancient times that people routinely cling to, will soon prove to be empty phrases; that is, the fine manner of speaking so much admired today, according to which children must be allowed to become what corresponds to their observed talents. This will soon prove to be an empty phrase. In the first place, people will see that those who are born from now on will give indications of their previous incarnations in a more complex way than was the case with people in the fourth post-Atlantean epoch. They will show complex potentialities that no one would have dreamed of before since these potentialities were far simpler in earlier times. Those who consider themselves especially clever in testing the potentialities of grown children to determine whether or not they are fitted for this or that vocation may learn that the insights derived from these tests are nothing but their own fantastic imaginations.

In the near future, however, life will be so complicated that the word profession will take on an entirely different meaning. Today we still often associate something quite inward with the word, calling it "vocation," although for most people their vocations do not at all represent anything inward. We conceive vocation (calling) as something toward which a person is called by his inner qualities. However, if we would question people about their calling, especially in our cities, many would say, "I am in my profession because I am convinced this is the only one that corresponds to my talents and inclinations that I have had since childhood." Yet, closer inspection of these cases would reveal that the answers given did not correspond with the facts, and I imagine they are not congruent with your own observation of life. Today, a vocation is increasingly that to which a person is called by the world's objective course of development. There outside of men is the organism, the interconnection; you may call it, if you please, the machine—this is not important—that gives orders, that calls him.

All this will constantly intensify and, as a result, what humanity accomplishes through vocational activity is also detached from man himself; it becomes more objective. Through this detachment, vocational activity grows increasingly into something that, in its further development through Jupiter, Venus, and Vulcan, goes through a process of development similar to what has taken place for the earth through Saturn, Sun, and Moon. It is a peculiar fact that when one speaks as a spiritual scientist it is not possible to flatter human beings if the subject is related intimately to their lives. Spiritual science will be less and less exposed,

77

you see, to the danger of expressing itself according to the model of wisdom to be found in the words:

> At best a pompous moralistic play
> With wonderfully edifying quips,
> Most suitable to come from puppets' lips.[67]

Spiritual science will certainly not be in a position to do this. It will often be compelled to set forth as something significantly great for the evolution of the world the very thing that people would prefer not to hear. It will therefore be inevitable that some people today who consider themselves exceedingly bright because their philistinism has crept into their brains will glibly declare, "Oh, professional life is a prosaic, mundane matter." The way vocational life appears to true spiritual science compels us to declare that through the very fact that this life becomes detached from human interests, it contains the necessity to develop relationships possessing a cosmic significance. Many people might think that a depressing view of the future results from this: increasingly people are caught in the treadmill of life and spiritual science cannot even console them that this has happened.

It would, however, be a great deception should one draw such a conclusion from what has been said since the nature of the universe requires things to be unified through polar opposites. Just consider how these polarities thrust themselves upon you in the world! It is, for example, in their mutual relationship that positive and negative electricity produce their unified effects. Positive and negative electricity are necessary to each other. Male and female are necessary for the propagation of the human race. It is from polarities that unity evolves in the evolution of the world.

Now, the same principle is at the bottom of what has been said. When vocational labor is separated from the human being, we necessarily create the first cosmic potentiality for a far-reaching cosmic evolution. Everything that happens in the evolution of the world is related to the spiritual, and in what we create within the sphere of our vocations, whether by bodily or by mental labor, there lies the possibility for the incarnation of spiritual beings. At present, during this earth stage, these spiritual beings are, to be sure, still of an elemental kind; we might say an elemental kind of the fourth degree. But they will have become elemental beings of the third degree during the Jupiter evolution, and so on. The labor in the objective vocational process is detached from us and becomes the external sheath for elemental beings who thereby continue their development. But this occurs only under a certain condition.

If it be said that we must first begin to understand the meaning of what is often belittled as the prosaic part of life, we must also understand that this meaning is not clarified until we comprehend it completely in its comprehensive cosmic connection. What we produce in our vocational life can become meaningful for the Vulcan evolution, but something else is prerequisite to this. Just as positive electricity is necessary for negative, and the male necessary for the female, so also what will be released continuously from humanity as activity will require an opposite pole. A polarity of opposites was also present for humanity in its earlier evolutionary stages. Something absolutely new, of course, does not come into existence here because something similar was already present before. But when you look back at earlier cultural periods, if only two or three centuries ago, you will find that the human being was still far more immersed in his professional life with his feelings and passions, in fact with all his emotions, than today. When you compare the joy that a human being could still experience in his or her profession even a hundred years ago with the dissatisfaction of many people today who have nothing but their profession, you will be able to form an impression of what really needs to be said.

79

Such things are really considered rightly far too infrequently for the simple reason that those who discuss the character and choice of vocation are those who can least afford to talk about this subject matter. Schoolmasters, literary scholars, parsons—the very people who least experience the dark side of vocational activity in the modern world—write about these things. Thus you will find in ordinary literature and even in pedagogical books that people express themselves on this subject like the blind discussing colors. Of course, someone who has finished elementary and high school, and then looked around a little in a university because that's the thing to do, may easily consider himself unusually clever with the ideas he has absorbed; that is, if he now plays the role of a reformer of humanity who can tell us how everything should be done. There are, indeed, many such individuals. A person who has gained a proper perception of life knows that they are the ones who usually talk most stupidly about what must come about. This is ordinarily not observed simply because those who have acquired such educational credentials are at present highly respected. The time is yet to come when the feeling will develop that the so-called men of letters, the journalists and narrowly educated schoolmasters, understand the interrelationships of life least of all. This must gradually develop as a general opinion.

It is important that we come to see more clearly how in earlier times man's emotional life was intricately related with his professional life and how subsequently the latter has increasingly become disengaged from man's emotional life and must continue to do so. For this reason, the polar opposite of vocational life must become something different from what it was earlier. What was this element that was added earlier to vocational life? You have it before you today when you consider what constitutes the shell of culture. The buildings in which professions are practiced and in the midst of these, the church, have become the sheath and shell of culture; the days of the week reserved for work, and Sunday reserved for the needs of the soul. These were the two poles: the vocational life and the life dedicated to religious conceptions.

It would be one of the greatest mistakes that could be made to suppose that this other pole as it is still conceived today by the religious denominations could remain as it is, since it was made to fit a vocational life still bound up with the emotions of men. All of human life will deteriorate unless understanding increases in this sphere. So long as the elemental spirit that an individual creates in his vocation, as I have described, was not separated from him, the old religious conceptions still sufficed to some extent. Today they are no longer sufficient, and they will become less so the farther we advance into the future. The very idea that is most vociferously opposed by certain people must be revived; that is, the opposite pole, consisting of the fact that men shall be able to form concrete concepts regarding the spiritual worlds, should enter into evolution.

The representatives of the religious sects will often say, "Oh, there they are in spiritual science talking about many spirits and gods, but it is the one God that is important; with Him alone we have enough." Thus, we can still make an impression on people today if we present them with the great advantage of coming into contact with one god, especially during after-dinner coffee and family music, when contemptuous remarks are made about other more recent endeavors, and ideas are expressed in an especially egotistic and philistine fashion. But what is really important is that human horizons should be broadened; that is, that we should learn to know that everything is permeated not just by a single divine spirit conceived in the vaguest way possible, but that spirit is also omnipresent in a concrete, special sense. People must learn to know that when a workman

81

stands at his vice and the sparks fly about elemental spirits are being created which pass over into the world process and there have their significance. Those especially clever ones will claim that this is stupid. These elemental spirits, however, will certainly come into existence even though the one working at the vice is unconscious of them. Nevertheless, they will still be created, and it is important that they shall come into existence in the right way since elemental spirits both destructive and helpful to the world process can come into being.

You will most clearly understand what I mean if you consider it in a special context because in all these things we are standing today at the threshold of new evolutionary developments. Many people already have an inkling of this. Should it be transformed into reality and people fail to have spiritual scientific aspirations, it would be the worst thing that could happen to the earth. What has come about primarily during the course of the fourth post-Atlantean epoch is that the human being has been liberated from the external, inorganic world which he embodied in his tools. Eventually, he will be reunited with what he has embodied in them.

Today, machines are constructed. Of course, they are at present objective, containing little of the human element. But it will not always be so. The course of the world tends to bring about a connection between what the human being is and what he produces and brings into existence. This connection will become ever more intimate. It will appear first in those areas that furnish the foundation for closer relations between one person and another—for example, in the treatment of chemical substances that are used in medicines. People still believe that when sulphur, oxygen, and some other substance—hydrogen or something else—have been combined, the product of this combination possesses only those effects that are derived from the individual substances. Today this is still true to a large extent, but the course of world evolution is tending toward something different. The subtle pulsations lying in the human being's life of will and disposition will weave and incorporate themselves gradually into what he produces. Thus, it will not be a matter of indifference from whom a certain preparation is received.

Even the most external and cold technical development tends toward a quite definite goal. Anyone who can form a vague conception of the future of technical development knows that an entire factory will operate in a completely individual way that will be in keeping with the one who directs it. His or her attitude of mind will enter into the factory and will pass over into the way in which the machines work. Human beings will blend with this objectivity. Everything that they touch will gradually come to bear a human impression. No matter how stupid it may seem today to the clever people—in spite of St. Paul having said that what men consider to be clever is often foolishness in the eyes of God[68]—people will realize that the time will come when an individual will be able to step up to a mechanism standing at rest and will know that to set it in motion he must move his hand this way, that way, and another way. Through the vibrations of the air caused by this signal, the motor[69], adjusted beforehand to respond to it, will be set in motion.

Then, national economic development will become such that to patent machines will be quite impossible; such things will be replaced by what I have just explained. Thus, everything will be excluded that has no relation to human nature, and by this it will be possible to bring about something quite definite. Just imagine what a truly good person who has reached an especially high level of morality will in future be able to do. He will construct machines with signals that can be governed only by individuals like himself. Evil minded people will produce quite different vibrations when they make these signals, and the machine will not respond.

83

People already have a faint inkling of this. It is not without purpose that I have called your attention to certain individuals who study flames dancing under the influence of definite tones. Further research in this direction will reveal the way to what I have just indicated. We might, indeed, say that it is the path back to those times when an alchemist who only wished to stuff money into his pocket could accomplish nothing, whereas another, who wished only to set up a sacrament for the glory of the gods and the welfare of humanity, would be successful.

In a sense, so long as what arose from human work bore the aura of the emotions and joys that men transferred into it, it was not accessible to the kind of influence that I have just described. But to the extent that the products of vocational labor can no longer be produced with special and absolutely necessary enthusiasm, what thus flows away from men and streams forth from them can become a motor force. The truth is that through the fact that individuals can no longer unite their emotions with the world of machinery, they, in a way, restore to this world the purity that arises from or serves their labor. In the future it will no longer be possible for people to bestow the warmth gained from the enthusiasm and joy derived from their work on the things produced. But these things themselves will be purer as they are put into the world by workers. They will also become more susceptible to what will emanate from, and be predetermined by, man as a motor force, as I have described.

Such a direction to human evolution can only be given by concrete knowledge of the spiritual forces that can be discovered by spiritual science. In order that this development may occur, it is necessary for an ever greater number of individuals in the world to gradually find the opposite pole. This consists in uniting one human being with another in what rises far above all vocational labor, while at the same time illumining and permeating it. Life in the spiritual scientific movement furnishes the foundation for a united life that can bind all professions together. If there were only an external advance of vocational evolution, this would result in a dissolution of human ties; people would become less able to understand one another or to develop relationships according to the requirements of human nature. They would increasingly disregard one another, seek only their own advantage, and have only competitive relationships with one another. This must not be permitted to come to pass lest humanity thereby fall into complete decadence. To prevent this from happening, spiritual science must be propagated.

It is possible to describe truly what many people are today unconsciously striving for, even though they deny it. There are many today, you know, who say, "This talk about the spiritual is ancient twaddle! The true advance that will really bring about human progress is to be found in the development of the physical sciences. When men get beyond all this twaddle about spiritual things, we will then, in a way, have a paradise on earth."

Should nothing prevail in humanity except competition and the compensatory acquisitive instinct, however, it would not be paradise on earth but hell. After all, there would have to be another pole if real progress were to take place. If a spiritual pole were not sought for, there would have to be an ahrimanic pole. Then the following argument would prevail: "Should vocations continue to be specialized, there would always be a certain unity in that one person would be this, another that, but all would have the common characteristic of acquiring as much as possible through their jobs." True, all would be made alike, but this is simply an ahrimanic principle. It is incorrect to think that the world can reach its goal through such a one-sided evolution, proceeding purely in the external sphere as we have described it. To follow this line of thinking would be tantamount to a woman's arguing that men had gradually become worse, were really utterly unfit for the world, and should be completely exterminated, and that then we would get the right evolution of the physical world.

It would require a weird person, indeed, to hold such a view since nothing whatever could be achieved by getting rid of all the men. Because this applies to the sensory world, people understand it, but they do not understand such foolishness in reference to the spiritual world. Yet, it is the same for spiritual relationships as if someone were to suppose that mere external evolution could continue to progress; it cannot. Just as the earlier evolutionary periods required the abstract religions, so this new stage requires a more concrete spiritual knowledge as it is striven for in the spiritual scientific movement. The elemental beings that are created and released through the vocational labor of men must be fructified by the human soul with what it takes into itself from impulses striving upward to the spiritual regions. Not that this is the only mission of spiritual science, but it is the mission related to the advancing and changing vocational life. Therefore, world evolution demands that as professions become more specialized and mechanized, people feel the need for the opposite pole to become proportionately more intensely active in them. This means that each human being should fill his soul with what brings him close to every other human being, no matter what their specialized work may be.

All this leads to much more. As we will hear in due course, a new age will emerge from what we may describe as our own time's indifference to and withdrawal from life, which is frequently the experience of working people these days. In the new age, human beings will again perform their work from different impulses. These will really be no worse than those good old vocational impulses that cannot be renewed, but must be replaced by others of a different sort. In this connection we can already point today, not merely abstractly but quite concretely, to a human ideal that spiritual science will develop. This will show what even a vocation may become to human beings when they understand how to observe the signs of the times in the right manner.

We shall continue our reflections regarding the significance of these matters for the individual, and for karma.

V

From these reflections on the segment of human life that is formed by, or associated with, a vocation, you will have seen that it is difficult to explain these things because they bring so much into consideration. We must bear in mind that everything that is brought into a life through the laws of destiny, of karma, depends on many factors, and the very multiplicity of life rests upon just this truth.

A special comment is in order here if, in the word vocation, we subsume individual human elements from a life's destiny. In other words, what is called the vocation of an individual must not be confused with what we designate, in the broadest sense, as his official position. It is obvious that all sorts of confusion would result if we directed our attention to what someone represents in his or her official position and subject this to the point of view of vocational life represented here. The very fact that people frequently have to follow their vocation within an official position causes the most complex external factors to have a bearing on their lives, and other karmic threads may, after a fashion, also weave into their vocational karmas.

To be sure, we are living today in a period that is being slowly transformed, but the things we must mention here relative to vocational karma are by no means the sole determinants in placing a person in this or that position in life. We know that today vocational karma is crossed in many ways by the karma of entire ranks and classes of human beings. The ambition, vanity, and prejudice of an individual, as well as the people around him, have a bearing on the many factors that influence the way he or she occupies a position in life within a group. All of them work into vocational karma from without and render it possible for ahrimanic influences to mingle continually in human activity. Someone in a certain position in life, who, through all sorts of means that are well-known and need not be mentioned, has become, let us say, a minister or councillor of state, does not necessarily have the mission (vocation) to occupy this post. Such a person may hold a high position, yet his or her mission may be that of a clerk, but we need not suppose that for this reason the position cannot be occupied. It is the peculiarity of our time that the materialistic interpretation of the basic assumptions, justifiable as they may be in themselves, has brought forward such a theory of life as that of the "selection of the fittest." Even Oskar Hertwig, the student of Haeckel[70] has criticized such an interpretation by pointing out that this age of ours which has produced such a doctrine clearly selects the least fit for the most important positions, and this to an extent that is unparalleled when compared to the total scope of life in other ages. We are not simply deprecating our own times in a pessimistic way and referring to the good old times that are past, but we stand here in the presence of an actual fact. The very people who take pride now in the theory of the selection of the fittest are the ones who in reality yield to the tendency of choosing the least qualified people for the seemingly most important places in life.

This is a bitter truth today. Yet, it would be recognized if the present age were not entirely under the influence of the most far-reaching faith in authority, stupor of opportunism, and dominated by what is called public opinion, which a philosopher of the nineteenth century termed "private foolishness." To repeat, people would see what is of real importance here if it were not for the immense influence of present public opinion that flows from such muddy sources.

We must, therefore, understand that our age has to be educated to a stronger grasp of life through learning to see that we are immersed in one-sidedness, in *the selection of the worst*. This must come to pass in spite of so-called public opinion and its hero worship of the least qualified people.

Official positions are often filled by Ahriman-Mephistopheles and, as the *Faust* unfolds, you can see how Mephistopheles attends to his official responsibilities. Faust was able to free himself from Mephistopheles only at the end of his life. He comes now to the King's palace and produces paper money—an invention of extraordinary importance for the last century. But it is Mephistopheles who really invents it. Faust is then guided into the ancient world by Homunculus, who had come into existence through the help of Mephistopheles. He even becomes a commander-in-chief and conducts wars, but in the presentation used by Goethe in this act, we can see that, in reality, Mephistopheles carries on these wars. In the end we see how Faust gradually frees himself from Mephistopheles. Even though Faust, after he has abandoned the professorship he previously held, simply roams about the world without having definite official position, we must say that Mephistopheles stands beside him in the way in which the Mephistophelian force plays into the life of humanity. This is one thing we must pay attention to.

A second fact is equally important. It is extremely difficult to properly investigate what really works in man's nature in the course of karmic evolution. Indeed, we may say that in this area, too, scientific development has arrived at a point where it must be replaced by spiritual scientific observation. It is precisely in dealing with the life of the soul that scientists make the most terrible blunders. Indeed, we observe that there is a perverted scientific school of thought that ventures to confront soul life by trying to observe it in a scientific way, admitting that it is not to be found in consciousness but that much of it rises up into consciousness from the unconscious or subconscious that lies below the threshold. In previous discussions we have presented concrete examples of soul life that really lie in the subconscious and rise up into consciousness like the clouds of smoke that are produced when bits of paper are burned in the region of a solfatara.[71] To be sure, a great deal lies below in the depths of consciousness.

We may say, then, that for a proper understanding of things some psychologists already presume it to be necessary to posit the presence or absence of an obscure, unconscious capacity in the soul. Since, however, they are not yet willing to adjust to a more comprehensive spiritual scientific conception of the world, they can produce only a caricature. A person holding the point of view of scientific psychology looks upon a human life as it has developed. To be sure, it is no longer supposed that what the soul feels and wills, what causes it happiness or unhappiness, joy or pain, depends only on what it has retained in consciousness. The effort is made now to quiz the soul to draw out of it what it has passed through in joy, sorrow, disillusionment in life and other things that have been forgotten. What has been forgotten, however, has not disappeared, so it is said, but has burrowed into the subconscious.

Especially the unsatisfied and subsequently suppressed appetites of an earlier time are said to agitate in the subconscious. Let us take the specific case of a woman in her thirtieth year. When she was sixteen, she fell in love, developing a genuinely erotic passion, which, so this scientific school says, would have led her life astray if she had surrendered to it and if it had been fulfilled. Under the influence of her education and the advice of her elders, however, she suppressed it—swallowed it, to use a trivial expression—down into her soul. She lives on and fourteen years pass. She is perhaps now married in keeping with her position in life. So far as her daily thinking and feeling are concerned, the matter is long forgotten; but what is forgotten has not disappeared. The content of the soul is not exhausted in what it knows, this school of thought would claim, and in the depths of her soul this incident is still present. But in spite of being outwardly happy, this lady suffers from an indefinable tendency toward pessimism, a partial weariness of life, from nervousness or neurasthenia, or something of the kind, and these symptoms are then diagnosed as an expression of her suppressed anxiety about the incident earlier in her life. The effort is then made to introduce this kind of psychology into the science of healing, to cure such souls through questioning. The patients are told that such experiences still reside in the deepest regions of the psyche, apparently forgotten by the upper level of consciousness, and that they must be drawn to the surface. If, under the influence of a skillful interrogator who, according to the views in vogue, must be a psychologist, they are thus brought to the surface, and if the person comes to understand the matter, then things will be better. Actual "cures" are frequently achieved by these means, although in most cases patients only seem to be cured. To what extent they are apparent cures, however, we can explain on some other occasion. This, then, is one example of how scientists try to penetrate the depths of the soul's life.

Another example has to do with a man thirty-five or forty, who is suffering from a certain weariness of life, from a certain vacillation in life. Neither he nor those about him know why, least of all he himself. Someone who deals with such a "science of the soul," as we have explained, then burrows into the forgotten subterranean soul life of this man and brings to light the fact that the plan he had for his life when he was about sixteen was wrecked. He then had to turn to a different plan, one that was unrelated to the other. Certainly he seems to have been content in what he felt, thought, and willed from one day to another, but this is not the entire life of the soul; the shattered plan of life still continued to be a living force in the deepest crevices of the soul.

In this case, too, the "experts" believe the man can be cured when, through questioning, this shattered plan of life is discovered and the person can come to an understanding of it through his questioner. It is also supposed that there is much in the depth of the soul that the consciousness knows nothing of. In short, the conclusion has been reached that consciousness represents only a small part of what comprises the life of the soul. But what people are now trying to find on the bottom of the soul's life is really some sort of soulless sediment. A theologian recently called it somewhat coarsely—"the bestial slime at the bottom of the soul." That is to say, disillusionments, suppressed appetites, ruined life plans, "the bestial slime at the bottom of the soul," all come from the lower depths of the soul life. This refers to everything that is rooted in the life of the flesh, the blood, the animalistic; it does not come from the soul's depths in a conscious way because consciousness would, and actually does, resist all this.

There is certainly some truth in this theory of the "bestial slime at the bottom of the soul." How often in life do we hear our consciousness say: "I really want only one thing; I would like to experience this or that, which is why I turn to this or that person." But the slime at the bottom begins to work, and it may be only bestial appetites that are at play, disguised by what the consciousness says. It is further maintained by this "scientific" school that these unconscious regions also harbor everything that is derived from the connection of the individual with race, nation and all sorts of other historical residues that play their roles unconsciously in the soul, while the consciousness itself is behaving quite differently. In view of all that is brewing in the world today, one couldn't even say that these things

93

cannot be confirmed by examples from all over the world. How could one deny that many people today speak of lofty ideals regarding the rights and freedom of a people while all that is really active in their souls is what burrows in the bottom slime, deriving from the connections psychoanalysis seeks to analyze.

Then the theological psychoanalysts—and I do not know how they and the scientific psychoanalysts reason with each other—also include the demonic as part of the subconscious life of the soul—in other words, that which emerges from still greater depths, the utterly irrational, as it is said. The theological psychoanalysts take great satisfaction especially in the thought that unknown demons work in the subconscious soul in order, for example, to change people into gnostics or theosophists. They think that when the soul has been psychoanalyzed, when we have penetrated its deepest regions where the "primeval slime" lies, a demonic teaching such as that of gnosis can be discovered there, or a demonic teaching such as that of psychoanalysis—excuse me, not psychoanalysis, which according to the view of these men and women is not to be found there, but theosophy and other things also mentioned in this connection. Well, I really did not want to enter into a criticism of psychoanalysis, but my purpose in explaining all this is to indicate that something in these psychonanalytical endeavors forces contemporary research into contact with what lies, works and weaves below the conscious part of the soul. Nonetheless, the most perverted findings must result from these endeavors because of the preconceptions of scientists and their unwillingness to take account of spiritual scientific investigations in this field. What they are able to discover in the life of the soul can only be analyzed in the right way with the knowledge that human life proceeds through repeated lives on earth. Yet the psychoanalysts attempt to explain what exists at the bottom of the soul on the basis of a single life on earth, and it is not surprising that the picture they paint is so highly distorted.

One who finds, for example, ruined life plans at the bottom of the soul must first investigate the significance of such a ruin in the total human life that passes through repeated lives on earth. He or she would then perhaps discover that certain aspects of such a total human life are also active in the subconscious and, as a matter of destiny, have actually hindered that particular life plan from coming to fruition. Such an individual would then observe that this ruined life plan in the depths of the soul is destined, not simply to cause illness in this incarnation, but also to be carried through the portal of death as a force in the life between death and a new birth, playing its true role only in the next life on earth. It may, indeed, be a necessity that such a ruined life plan should at first be preserved in the depths of the soul where it may be strengthened and thereby enabled to gain its true form between death and a new birth so that it may take on the shape predestined for it in the next earthly life; this it could not have done in this present earthly life because of other characteristics in the soul's life.

So the "bestial slime at the bottom of the soul"—as I have said, the expression is disagreeable—is there, to be sure; but bear in mind what I have said regarding the relationship between the head and the rest of man's organism. His body is connected with his earthly life—indeed, with his present incarnation in many respects—whereas his head is the result of earlier stages of the evolution of the earth and is connected especially with his preceding incarnations. When you take this into consideration, you will understand that from the rest of the organism, in accord with the role that it plays in the entire karmic connection, much works upward that must possess a different stage of maturity from what comes from the head and nervous system. But one who merely analyzes the slime at the bottom in the psychoana-

95

lytic way is utterly misled. He is like a person who wishes to know what kind of grain will grow in a particular soil before grain has been grown there. In analyzing the soil he finds a certain manure with which it has been fertilized. So he says, ''Now I know the manure from which the next crop of grain will grow.'' The grain does not by any means grow from the manure, in spite of the fact that it must be there! The essential thing is what is planted in this mud at the bottom. This is often predestined to exert its influence through the portal of death into the next development on earth. What is needed is not to investigate the bestial bottom slime, but what is planted in this muddy substance as the seed of the soul.

So-called psychoanalysis makes possible investigations in the very region where present preconceptions are working in a disastrous fashion; we are dealing here with a field from which present thinking tends strongly to take its directions, since it is not content with what conscious experiences give to the soul. The general area in which research ought to be done is no longer in dispute, but because people who cannot understand spiritual science have no true guidelines for their investigations, they burrow aimlessly in the fields assigned them through their official connections or their own agitation. They do this in the most unskillful manner, placing everything in a false position because they do not know better. Their research would yield the proper results only if they were able to follow the true karmic threads, as I have indicated at least suggestively through reference to one thing and another. This psychoanalysis is terribly unsound, especially when it stirs up the region of the elemental. Yet it is of great importance to investigate fine and intimate formations of the threads reaching into the future destiny of a human being. What takes place in a person's conscious life from waking until sleeping reveals little of those forces that continue to work as a karmic stream through various incarnations. What we experience consciously during our waking life belongs largely to the present incarnation. It is well that it is so because we should be industrious in our present incarnation. But much that will be carried through the portal of death as a germ formed from the experiences of our present incarnation—the incidents through which we have passed, the proficiencies achieved—all this plays a significant role in our life from the moment of falling asleep to that of waking, and this often influences our dreams. We must learn, however, to judge the formation of dreams in the right way. When people say that they are reminiscences, this is often true, but they do not act in the stream of our karma in a linear fashion. In fact, they often act in such a way that their significance is the exact opposite of what they are represented to be. I will give you an example from literature in order to bring out clearly what I wish to say.

The aestheticist Theodor Vischer[72] included in his novel *Auch Einer* a clever little story that I will introduce here because I am speaking of vocational life in a more comprehensive way, that is, including everything that is connected with one's occupation. So I will give an illustration of this. In Vischer's novel, there is a conversation between a father and his son. They are walking together and, after the father has questioned his son about all sorts of things, the boy says, "Just think, the teacher told us that we should always ask what a person's occupation is because to have a proper occupation is important. In this way it is possible to learn whether or not the person is respectable and whether he has a good soul life." "I see," says the father. "Yes, indeed, and after the teacher told us this I had a dream in which I was walking by the lake over there and in my dream I asked the lake what sort of occupation it had, and the lake answered, 'I have the occupation of being wet.' " "Is that so?" says the father.

This is a most clever anecdote and one that reveals that the person who thought it out had much knowledge of life.

The father said, "Is that so?" because he naturally did not wish to confuse his son and tell him what a stupid thing the teacher had said. But that father no doubt had his thoughts on the subject. He really should have enlightened his son in a more intelligent way than the teacher had done, and should have said to him, "We should not form our judgments so superficially. It might well be that a person would be wrong as to what a respectable occupation is and might falsely consider a man to be disreputable; he might also be disadvantaged in some way." In short, the father would have had to correct his son, but in this particular case it was not necessary. The boy was still young, and his dream could still work in a favorable manner on him. This dream worked in his subconscious, but in such a way as to erase the stupidity of the teacher from his soul. Thus, the dream took on a form in the boy's subconscious, which is cleverer than the superficial consciousness, in such a way that a breath of ridicule was spread over the stupidity of the teacher. The lake said its occupation, its vocation, was to be wet. This is something that will work in a wholesome way in expelling the harmful influences of such teaching. Here the dream is a reminiscence that comes the very next night, but it also serves as a corrective in life. In fact, the astral body often works in this way, and we might find, together with the residue remaining in the soul from living experiences, particularly from wrongful instruction, that a corrective is also present in the subconscious forces of the soul. This often produces its influence even in the same incarnation in young people. Above all, however, its influence is carried through the portal of death and continues further. This constitutes a means of self-correction in man, and we must pay attention to this fact.

In mentioning these things I simply wanted to indicate how much there is in a human soul and how this forces its way from one incarnation into the next. We have to do with a whole complex of forces that project from one incarnation into another. Now we must consider what relationship exists between this complex of forces and the human being insofar as his life flows along between birth and death. Here he or she is really an instrument with four strings—physical, etheric, astral bodies, and ego—on which this bow of karmic forces plays its tune. The individual life comes into being according to the measure in which one or the other—the etheric body, the astral body, or the etheric together with the ego—is swept by the bow of karma, if you allow this comparison with a violin. The tones of these four strings of life may interplay in many ways, making it difficult to speak of and decipher, not in mere empty abstractions but in lithic detail, the individual life-melodies of human beings. Thus, it is possible to decipher them only when one is able to see how the bow of karma plays upon the four strings of a human being. However, general points of view come into consideration here, and to these we must turn our attention.

If we observe a human being in those years when, as explained in my brochure *The Education of the Child in the Light of Anthroposophy*, the physical body and especially the etheric body are primarily coming into development, if we observe the development of children from approximately the seventh to the fourteenth years, we shall note that just at this time certain characteristics appear in them that are especially typical of this period. Certain things consolidate themselves in a way, although many things overlap one another so that much that appears during the first seven years can be more thoroughly and profoundly observed only between the seventh and the fourteenth. It will be found that something appears in a more definite way in the developing child that we may call, in a sense, the inner peculiarities that are consolidated through the character and demeanor of the corporeality. This is so, however, only insofar as they come to expression in the posture and gestures of the physical being, and in the entire bearing of his life. I refer to what is there taking solid form; not all, to be sure, but a great part of what causes a human being to be stocky and short, or to have a taller body that causes him or her to walk in a particular way such as with a firm step or a dancing gait, to mention radical contrasts. As I have said, not all, but a great part of what thus appears in the developing child is derived from karma and is the effect of the vocation of his preceding incarnation. Mistakes are often made when no attention is paid to what I have just said; that is, when, to appear clever, an effort is made to determine what a child's vocation will be from his manner and bearing. He would thus, however, mistakenly be given a vocation similar to that of his previous incarnation, and this would be detrimental to the child.

When this period of a child's life ends, or even before that time because, as I have said, things overlap one another, then the astral body manifests itself in a special way by working back on what had been developed previously. If one realizes this and has derived it from spiritual science, it can then be observed also on the physical plane. In accordance with other karmic forces, the astral body works back in such a way that it transforms what had resulted from the purely vocational karma during the seventh to the fourteenth years. In other words, two antagonistic forces struggle with each other in the child. One group of forces gives him form; these come more from the etheric body. The other group, coming more from the astral body, works against these and in part paralyzes them, so that he is compelled to transform what has been forced upon him by the vocational karma of his previous incarnation. In other words, we may say that the etheric body works in a formative way; that is, what is manifested as the bearing of the physical body, as one's carriage, is derived from the etheric body. The astral body works in a transforming way.

Through the interplay of these two forces, which are really in bitter conflict with each other, much comes to expression that has to do with the working of vocational karma.

This now works together with other karmic currents, however, since we must also consider the physical body. With it, what comes primarily into consideration during the first period of life is how the human being has placed himself in the world by means of his karma. Even the kind of physical body we have depends upon this since, by reason of our karma, we place ourselves in a certain family in a specific nation. Thus, we receive a definitely formed body, but this is not all. Just think how much depends on the course of our life and on the situation into which we have entered by placing ourselves in a certain family. By that fact alone the basis is given for much in our life. As a matter of fact, during the first seven years in which the physical body is especially developing, forces are active in it—or we had better say around it—that are derived not from our vocation and all that was related to it in our previous incarnation, but from the way in which we have lived with others in previous incarnations. By this I mean how we stood in this or that relationship with this or that person during a preceding incarnation, not in any particular part of our life—this belongs to another field—but throughout our entire lifetime. Our souls work on this because they are profoundly affected by the relationships we had with human beings, and we bear with us what evolves from this process through the portal of death. Because of these forces, we bring it about that we place ourselves again in a certain particular family and situation in life. So we may say that what actually places our physical body here, in a sense, and works through it, also determines our situation in life. This continues to work further, of course, through the following lives, and meets its counterbalancing force through the ego. The ego works in a dissolving way upon life situations, but it also works in conflict with what is already determined in them. We may, therefore, say: Physical body, creative of the life situation; ego, transformative of the life situation. Through the united action of these two in this struggle, another current of karma takes hold of life since two forces are omnipresent in an individual: those that tend to keep him in a particular situation, and those that tend to disengage him from it.

1. Physical body: creative of the life situation
2. Etheric body: formative
3. Astral body: transformative
4. Ego: transformative of the life situation

That is to say, 1 and 4 work in a primary way upon one another, as do 2 and 3; but all four also work in the most manifold ways upon each other. The way we enter into relationships with new human beings during our life according to our karma depends upon the connection of 1 and 4 with each other. But this is to be traced back, in turn, to our relationships in earlier lives. The way we find our relationships in our daily work, our vocation, is connected with 2 and 3 and their reciprocal action upon each other.

I ask that you reflect upon all this for the present. We shall continue this study.

VI

You have seen how involved the more profound questions of destiny are in human life, something we recognize when we try to approach them in ways made possible by spiritual science. For this, however, many things today will be necessary if man is to correctly put himself into the nature of those phenomena that lead to a truly fruitful grasp of life. When we consider these involved problems, we must frequently take roundabout paths in order to see clearly the difficulties that hinder our understanding. We have all grown up, in a sense, in the thinking of the present, and even though many of us suppose we have attained to unprejudiced thinking, it is always well to be quite unsparing in testing ourselves and our self-knowledge, especially the unprejudiced character of our thinking. Before we proceed further, therefore, permit me to draw your attention to some particulars.

It is often difficult to discuss these things because language is obstinate when we undertake to work out concepts in accord with reality. It is easy to suppose that a concept that has been worked out and is, as it were, obtained from the sum total of occult science is directed toward an entirely different objective than is really intended. In this way, various misunderstandings arise. A certain observation may frequently be made when we discuss the course of life of eminent personalities. I will give you an example. A small brochure has just been published in Switzerland. It deals with the person we have mentioned in a different connection, Friedrich Theodor Vischer, the author of *Auch Einer* and the great *Aesthetics*, and describes with loving devotion the life of this true-hearted and extraordinarily prolific Swabian. Permit me to mention him here simply as an example of some things that we desire to consider in connection with the question of human destiny; we could just as well select another example.

Vischer was as true a Swabian by nature as might be found in the nineteenth century. The biographical sketch[73] that has just been published shows how he grew up in poverty, how this compelled him to take the theological training in the Tübingen seminary, and so on. Now, the point that interested me is that at the very beginning attention is called to the fact that even his secondary schooling was rather narrow. To be sure, the boys learned to get along in Latin and later in the Greek writers, but they really did not know until a rather late age into what main river the Neckar empties, nor had they even seen a map until they were fairly well along in years. Many such defects in the educational system are mentioned.

Now let us look at the matter in the right light. Friedrich Theodor Vischer became, in a sense, a great and famous man who accomplished something important. We must understand how he became the specific individual we find in history. The fact that he had never seen a map before a particular age has something to do with this; if he had seen a map earlier, a certain trait in his character would not have been present. Much else that is severely criticized had to be so. In short, if we view the matter from a more comprehensive standpoint, we shall say that the soul of Vischer descended from the spiritual world and chose precisely his environment. It wanted to have just the education that would keep it for a time from seeing a map. Likewise, his soul wanted to be close to the Neckar river but did not wish to know into which major river it emptied. If we study Vischer, we shall see that precisely all his whims and abundant peculiarities are truly integrating components of his greatness. So it seems really out of order for someone to write his biography and criticize the school that actually made him the very man he was.

Let it be clearly understood that I did not want to emphasize that schools which do not show maps to children are of the right kind. But for Vischer it was entirely right and had to be so. We have often experienced this in the nineteenth century and up to the present day. Certain famous scientists are a case in point. They were quick to criticize the present system of education, demanding that much more natural science be introduced into the schools. However, when someone would ask the scientists: "You yourselves experienced these conditions—do you find them so terribly bad," they generally did not know what to say. We must understand clearly that everything has at least two and, under some circumstances, many sides. What do we have really when a biographer sits down and so forms his concepts and ideas—in this case the biographer was a woman—that such a thing is written as I have just told you about Vischer? It really contributes nothing whatever to an understanding of the personality concerned. When someone forms such concepts, he actually slashes—spiritually, I mean—into the person with whom he is dealing. If we do not wish to slash into a personality with our concepts, we should simply have to characterize in a loving way the nature of the school in all its narrowness and how it brought forth this individuality. But people slash—and criticize, which is surely slashing in many respects. What is the cause of this?

It comes from cruelty, a quite definite characteristic that is widespread in the thought system of the present and is rooted in the subconscious. Since people lack the courage to practice this cruelty outwardly, they are cruel in their concepts and ideas. In many works of the present time we observe this cruelty in descriptions and representations. We observe it in much that is done and said, and it is far more common at the bottom of the soul than is ordinarily supposed. I have told you that in some schools of black magic the custom exists of acquiring the means for performing black magic by having the novitiate cut into the flesh of living animals. Certain characteristics are thus developed in the soul. Not everyone can do that at present, but many people gratify the same lust through their system of concepts; this does not lead to black magic, of course, but to our present civilization. Much today is permeated by this characteristic; of this we must be entirely clear. We arrive at an unprejudiced grasp of the world only by paying attention to such things; it is achieved in no other way.

Today, beginnings tending toward attaining a particular view of the relationships of the fifth post-Atlantean epoch do exist everywhere. We do not come to understand this period when we simply criticize it or surrender to an abstract idealism, without taking into consideration that what appears in the form of mechanism, as a mechanistic culture, belongs absolutely and necessarily to it. Merely to condemn the mechanical element has no meaning whatever. Now, beginnings toward some understanding of what gives continuing life to our fifth post-Atlantean epoch have actually appeared, but few concepts that correspond with reality have yet been found for it and there is little inclination to pay attention to those who have tried to grasp it. It will be necessary for us to deal with these people whose endeavors will be a point of departure for true energetic, spiritual scientific activities.

There is a significant poet of the fifth post-Atlantean epoch through whose poetic works the life of the age pulses. This is Max Eyth,[74] who ought to be better known because he is truly a poet of our epoch. He is also a Swabian, the son of a schoolmaster who wanted his son also to be a

106

schoolmaster but karma willed otherwise. Relatively early in his life he chose a technical vocation, became a true technician, and then went abroad to England. There he devoted himself especially to the production of steam-ploughs and became their poet. The way he has sung with warm, loving heart of these amazing mechanical beasts is today's true poetry. There is a peculiar interplay of sentiment in this heart. On the one hand, he is a man fully devoted to technology; on the other, he is receptive to everything that can be grasped without preconceptions by an intellect schooled in the mechanistic-materialistic concepts of the fifth post-Atlantean epoch.

Max Eyth wrote a novel which deals with the modern life of Egypt, where the English company that employed him frequently sent him to introduce and test the steam-ploughs. This novel contains an explanation of how the pyramids were built according to a specific system. Now, if you calculate certain ratios that Eyth discovered and included in a supplement to one of his novels, you will find, up to the thirtieth decimal point at least, the so-called number,[75] π, by which the diameter of a circle must be multiplied in order to arrive at the circumference. You understand: 3.14159 . . . carrying many decimals and extending to infinity. It might easily be supposed that this symbol π represents the result of later scientific progress. However, it occurred to Max Eyth that the ancient Egyptian temple priests must have known it up to the thirtieth or fortieth decimal point in primeval times because they used it to determine the ratios according to which they built the pyramids. In other words, because Eyth was a technician, something was disclosed to him that is deeply hidden in the ancient structure of the pyramids. Thus he was able to point out that our culture really has two origins: the one that we know from historical records and that of ancient times in which people depended on a kind of knowledge that relied

107

more on atavistic clairvoyance; this later disappeared and today must be found again.

But still other things are to be found in Max Eyth. However insignificant it seems, this is extraordinarily important. One of his stories, a collection of which is entitled *Behind the Plow and Vice*, brings you face to face with a riddle of life, a riddle of destiny. It contains a splendid description of an engineer's capacities and ability to build bridges. But he is a little too brilliant; one might say, a bit careless. After he has built a bridge, which is again described in a splendid way, he is in a train passing over the bridge. There he sits in the train, but he has overlooked something in building the bridge. As he passes over it, it collapses and he is killed. This is an impressive karmic question—not answered, naturally, but posed. We see here how modern man approaches the profound question of destiny. Here we have a man who is brilliant in his profession and who dies at a relatively early age through his connection with a work that he created. I should like to say that this poetic fiction raises an important question of a sort that spiritual science seeks to answer. Such things do, of course, happen in the numerous variations of life. Now we have described a case that shows us how karma is fulfilled swiftly and precipitously. To be sure, such an event makes karma inevitable, but let us suppose hypothetically that in another case the person was not on the train as it passed over the bridge, but was sitting at home by the fire. Then he would probably have been imprisoned for a couple of years because of his mistake, but not much more than that would have happened to him in this life. What then?

You see, the important point is that what had brought death to this man, the death he suffered in connection with his work, must enter his karma either here in this life or in the life between death and a new birth. The experience must be gone through, but it may be accelerated as in the

108

case described by Eyth, or it may be extended over a longer period of time. Indeed, life itself in the fifth post-Atlantean epoch will raise profound questions of destiny and the very conditions of life in this epoch will make people realize how life reveals riddles in a new way that is different from that of earlier epochs.

Thus, when we consider people who are really somewhat gifted with brilliant intellects, we can observe that they seek today for different complexities of life in their artistic creation than those of earlier periods. How frequently it happens that the individuals who do discover significant complexities of life are those who are engaged in practical vocations. From this point of view the books of Max Eyth are extraordinarily instructive: first, because he is really a great and gifted writer, and second, because, as an entirely modern human being, he creates wholly from the requirements of modern life. It is especially interesting—permit me to make this remark parenthetically—that those who read Eyth learn through this mere outward exposure much that it would be important for theosophists to know—for example, many things connected with the life of Olcott,[76] the first president of the Theosophical Society. We find this hidden away in the writings of Eyth, who was in America at a time when Olcott was doing all kinds of strange things there. In short, even social karma may thrust itself upon us when we do not disdain acquainting ourselves with what this modern spirit has written. In general, however, the peculiar fact is that often not the individuals gifted with genius—Max Eyth was a genius—but those formed by the life-mechanisms of the fifth post-Atlantean epoch, see the intricacies of modern life with special clearness because their minds are formed in a special way.

I am acquainted with a man who was a jurist in his younger years[77]—a time when one could be a legal mind without necessarily realizing his financial gains from the practice of law. He was a clear-headed person who viewed everything without preconceptions, who by reason of his gifts attracted the attention of his superiors, as one calls them, not so much on account of his brilliance, but because he was a good and diligent worker whom they could use. Now, since he had established his reputation as an actuary or assessor, he entered a government ministry where he was also a remarkable worker who viewed everything with open eyes. There he was once assigned an important, significant task. He was to prepare a report on matters pertaining to the schools and to education and he was instructed to prepare it in such a way that it would indicate a transition to a sort of liberal system. That pleased him and, since he was a clear-headed individual who saw through the present state of affairs, an excellent report resulted, really an excellent plan of reform that looked to liberalizing and modernizing some of the conditions in the schools. But while he was working on his report, the market changed, as people say, and a reactionary report was required. His superior then said to him, "This report is so good that you certainly will be able to prepare a comparable reactionary report also; now, can you do this?" The man replied, "No, that I cannot do!" "Indeed, why not?" "Because this report presents my conviction!" "What? This is your conviction?" Well, the superior was most indignant and saw quite clearly that he no longer had any use for this man, a person not only diligent but also possessed of a conviction of his own. Clearly, such a person could not be used.

Yet, the man was an excellent jurist and worker. What could be done? He had proven himself everywhere, and it was well known that he was a competent jurist. Well, the effort was made to give him a promotion. People who have proven themselves in this way must, if possible, be kept contented. Things were arranged a little behind the scenes, as the expression goes, and one day—I think it was at a game of skittles—the secretary of a theater met this person as if by chance and said to him, "Do you know that the position of director of an important theater is vacant?" Now, the jurist, who had been attached to a government ministry, could not take it amiss when he was given this news. So when the game was over, the secretary said to him, "Won't you join me at the coffee house so I can explain the matter in detail? Would you like to be a theater director? We need one, but we cannot know, of course, when we select someone whether he would want the position under present conditions." Then the jurist, who was quite intelligent and well versed in juristic matters and things pertaining to administration, replied, "Of course, that simply has to be accepted. One must be willing and, if one is not, he will simply be arrested." Now, the end of the affair was that the position of director of the theater was offered him. There was one difficulty, however. There was a famous actress connected with the theater and whoever was to become the director had to be acceptable to her. "Well now," said the secretary, "can you also get along with this actress?" "Oh, if that's all that's required! I have been in a theater no more than seven times in my life but, if I take this job, I shall certainly be able to get along with her. Can you tell me what she likes to eat?" Now, the other knew that her favorite food was poppyseed cake. That was lucky. He said, "We will go at once to the bakery and order a large cake for her." This was delivered early the next morning. In the afternoon the secretary called on the actress in order—well, I suppose to sound her out, as the expression goes. He knew that she had a good deal of influence so he said to her. "We should like very much to have this gentleman as director. What do you think of him?" "Well," she answered, "I don't know him at all, but so far he has only been good to me." So the jurist became the director of the theater.

Well, the most famous critic of that city still had to be

won over. He was always writing the most terrible stuff until one day he also was brought around—at least, to such an extent that even if he did not write approvingly of the director, he did not disapprove either. This came about in the following way. I am not telling you a fairy story but something that actually happened; I only wish to describe it to you. So, the most highly placed person connected with the theater, even above the director, did not know what to do because of the critic. The new director was simply there, and he gave a good account of himself, being just as competent as the director of the theater as he had previously been as a jurist. But their top executive simply did not know what to do. He could not discharge the director, but the critic kept up his clamor. What did he finally do? He invited both of them in and served them some good wine. The director could drink and drink and drink. So could the critic, but not to equal the director. So it happened that early the following morning—about five o'clock, I think—the director rang the critic's doorbell and said he had to speak to his wife because he had left something quite heavy down below on the steps that he had to deliver to her. Well, she put on her dressing gown and he delivered her husband to her, a veritable bundle of misery. From that very hour the criticism decreased. Later, after this man had gone too far as a theater director in the view of his superiors, he was once more helped to a promotion in the legal profession.

Now, this man described in a remarkable way what he had observed in his occupation, and I wish only to show by this example that those people who are involved in the actual life of the present can make quite significant comments on it.

Still more interesting is a similar man, but one of nobler attitude than the one I have just mentioned, who wrote various things during his life. Shortly before his death—everyone of whom I am speaking is no longer alive—he produced a very interesting novella, really a contemporary work of art. Just think how anyone can write such a short story today according to the taste of the age. There must be nothing spiritual in it and, if there is, it must be pointed out quite clearly that the reader may believe the story or not; or better, he may consider it to be merely a fable. Now, I will present the material for the story, which this writer found in contemporary life. A person lived in the same environment as the man whom I have previously described. For a number of years he belonged to the legal profession and was relatively successful. The novelist can describe this. He can show how this character passed through the stages of his career as a jurist, how he had this or that experience and underwent complications of one kind or another. Then he can weave a love story into this material; of course, that also is the modern way. That is, the writer can tell how an exotic young lady comes to the jurist accompanied by her mother, how this eminent jurist falls in love with her and how, because a theme of espionage is introduced and he has to deal with this as a judge, he is again brought into relationship with the young lady. This brings him into a conflict, and so on. The story may then relate quite realistically how he is finally led to commit suicide.

The writer to whom I refer, however, did not do this; he wove the following significant material into his story. He narrated a course of events that is outwardly almost the same as I have told you, but he also lets the jurist read Schopenhauer and other philosophers in such a way that their thoughts, I might say, become totally enmeshed with his individual being, if not his nervous system. Now, he is a competent jurist. What does it mean when one, as a judge, is a competent jurist? It means such a person must be able to discover all possible hair-splitting subtleties in order to bring about a defendant's undoing, and he must likewise discover all possible legal casuistries of the defense. In short, this jurist is extraordinarily competent, and he convicts a certain person in a set of circumstances similar to those I have just described. But the defendent in the story behaved in a most astonishing way during the trial—that is, as if demonic—and especially the look in his eyes remained unforgettable in the minds of the people who were present during the trial. Well, the person concerned was, of course, imprisoned. The whole affair was then associated with that young lady with whom the judge had fallen in love. The convicted man, who was in ill health, was sentenced to twenty years in the penitentiary.

The judge is exceedingly well described in this story. He had not thought of the convict since the trial, which people thought he had conducted brilliantly, when one night he awoke at about twelve o'clock. He lay only half asleep. At about two o'clock there was a knock at the door of the room and the convict entered. You can imagine the situation, but he nevertheless fell again into a half-sleep and when he awoke, it was already day. He was now seized with a terrible fear. He went to the court; once, on the way to his chambers he heard the name of the convict called out. This terrified him tremendously. He decided to study the documents again and had them brought to him. But he left them lying there for three weeks. Finally, in a conversation one day it was revealed that about two o'clock on a certain night the convict had died in the penitentiary. It was precisely the time, as the judge could establish, when the prisoner had visited him in his bedroom!

This is the plot of the story, which is called *Hofrat Eysenhardt* and in which the judge finally commits suicide. *Hofrat Eysenhardt* by Berger[78] is an entirely modern story and shows even through other descriptions that the author was quite familiar with various recent endeavors to penetrate the secrets of occult existence. From this point of view alone the story is brilliantly written.

Now, there is something extraordinary here. Berger is

not the same writer I previously described; I introduced him only as an example of a man whose perception was incisive and who described well the very nerve of the fifth post-Atlantean epoch. I brought in this Berger as an official colleague, so to speak. Alfred Baron von Berger wrote that remarkable story, *Hofrat Eysenhardt*; it is written in such a way that we see he understands the various endeavors today to enter the spiritual world. Berger wrote much during the course of his life, but he published this story only after he had attained a position beyond which he could make no further progress. We may say this occurred "by chance" shortly before his death. This is most significant since it shows us that today whose who wish to get somewhere, as the expression goes, believe they make a mistake when they become involved in such things. But it also shows us how the striving of men tends in the direction of penetrating the mysterious aspects of existence. These aspects will increasingly come to the fore because they set important riddles before man.

If we wish to consider the question of destiny without presuppositions, we must first acquire a clear perception and try not to sleep through life—excuse the bald expression—but rather look around ourselves. Let me express figuratively the important point to bear in mind. Let us say that we have here one stream of life, there a second, there a third, since life consists of many streams crossing one another in the most manifold ways—for example, the life of the individual and that of groups of people, as well as the life of all humanity. The sort of concepts that dominate today are entirely too simplistic to disentangle the intertwining threads of life. Frequently, what needs to be done is to direct one's gaze first toward one point, then another, and then to relate these two points through one's perception. When we thus hit upon the right facts, the situation is then illumined.

Now, you will say, "Yes, but how can such things be accomplished?'' Well, that is just the point. When you pursue spiritual science in the right way, your imagination will reveal to you those points in life that you must consider together, so that life may unveil itself to you. By contrast, if you simply trace the consecutive events of life, you will understand nothing whatever of its totality. This is the way the historians do, in a sense; they draw threads from one event to another but do not understand life at all because what is needed is to view the world symptomatically. This will become increasingly necessary; that is, to view the world in such a way that we direct our perception to the right places and then draw the lines of connection from them to other things. A clear, symptomatic view of things is especially important in the concrete study of karma—with which so much is associated that is confusing because so much is seductive in it.

   I have already pointed out[79] that some contemporary occult societies have endeavored to keep this symptomatic study as far as possible from human beings. I have called your attention to the societies that are derived from ancient institutions and still continue to call themselves ''occult,'' especially in Western Europe. Within these occult societies special study has been devoted to human character in order to be able to use and grasp these characteristics in the right way. All sorts of ways have been used to keep this knowledge, which is fostered within their walls, from the rest of humanity. When the connection between the occult endeavors of these modern societies and public events are some day laid bare, when the threads are exposed that lead from them to modern events and their methods are exposed, it will be exceedingly interesting. These occult societies had a way of dealing with human characters by taking in hand the threads of their karma, guiding and directing them without their being conscious of this. Simple attempts have often been made in the Theosophical Society, but they have remained for the most part dilettantish because the theosophists lacked the skills of other occult societies. It is, of course, difficult to speak about these things, especially today when an objective characterization is not only suppressed by prejudice but is even forbidden by law. It is difficult to speak of these things; indeed, in a certain sense, it is quite impossible. But intimations must be given in one way or another since it is impossible for people simply to live and share in all that flows from the karma of the age into the unconscious region of their souls and then, in spite of living in this nebulousness, also to cultivate spiritual science, which demands clear and unprejudiced minds. There must be truth in certain things, but it is not possible to gain the truth in an abstract way by hypocrisy when we have to do with things that pertain to the real occult world. What is essential is that we must have a real will to truth. Now, this will to truth meets with many obstacles, especially today because men have gradually lost their sense for it. Just think how often in public life people are not concerned with discovering the truth, but rather with saying whatever suits one person or another and offers certain advantages to them.

Nowadays one comes upon particular fields everywhere of which it is not possible to speak, even though it is so necessary to do so. But I ask you to give the most earnest attention to this very fact because we must understand quite clearly that what has been said is the truth. You may ask, "What have these things to do with the question of karma we are now discussing?" Indeed, they have much to do with this, and we shall undertake to go into some of them in order finally to reach the goal toward which we are really striving.

VII

It is now my task to explain, episodically in a sense, something that is related directly to the practical and general outward life of humanity, in order to cast light on the direct relation to life that is essential to spiritual science in our time. I hope we shall still come to the parts of our lectures that have more to do with the inner life. As a whole, the central concern of our present considerations is to attain a spiritual scientific understanding of the position of the individual human being in practical, even vocational, life. *On The Karma of Vocation* is the title I should like to give these lectures I have been giving for some time. Thus, it is necessary to gain a broader basis, and so I must explain in a more comprehensive sense much that is related to the questions we are discussing.

We have made it clear that what the human being achieves for the world in any vocation is by no means something to be set aside as being prosaic, but that, as we have seen, it is most intimately related with his remote cosmic future. Each person integrates himself in a way into the social order of life. Because of his karma he or she is impelled to a certain vocation, none of which is to be considered more prosaic or poetic than the other, and we know that what a person accomplished within the social order is the first germ of something destined not only to have significance for our earth, but to evolve as the earth passes through the states of Jupiter, Venus, and Vulcan. What may be called an understanding of vocation, a knowledge of the significance of the immediate life, may truly dawn upon us through such reflections. It is precisely the mission of our spiritual scientific endeavors not merely to communicate pleasant sounding theories. Rather, we must let our souls be touched by what is suitable to place us correctly in life so that each person is in his or her own place in accordance with the spirit of our age, with the arché[80] of our time. Thus, our truths bear a character that is always strong enough to constitute the basis for a real judgment of life. We will not revel in comforting conceptions, but will take in those that will carry us through life.

When we recall something I have frequently emphasized, we shall see that even our scientific endeavors have the tendency to touch our souls with what is really meaningful for life. I have often called your attention to a significant fact that may, in a relatively short time, perhaps play a most important scientific role if only those whose mission is to cultivate learning are not too obtuse. A great deal of emphasis is placed today on the role heredity plays in human life, and teachers who talk about the vocations a person is destined to have also mention inherited characteristics when they wish to pass judgment on those things related to the future vocation of a person just entering life. Of course, they are just parroting what constitutes the current scientific view of the world. But those discussing the problem of heredity today mean that children inherit certain characteristics from their parents and ancestry strictly in a physical sense. External science cannot yet open its mind to a recognition of repeated earth lives and the carrying over of human characteristics from previous incarnations. People talk about heredity, but a correct opinion of it will be attained only when we introduce something that can be understood when we grasp the content of my little book, *The Education of the Child in the Light of Spiritual Science*.[81] There we see that human life first passes through a period of seven years, approximately to the change of teeth; a second period to the

119

fourteenth year; a third to the twenty-first, and so on all the way to the twenty-eighth year. Something more thorough on this subject may be found also in a small brochure that contains the substance of my lecture delivered a short time ago in Liestal,[82] in which I wished to call attention again, from another point of view, to these truths of the division of human development between birth and death into seven-year periods. We know that, in essence, the physical body develops inwardly between birth and the change of teeth, that the etheric body develops up to puberty, and that the astral body then passes through its development.

Let us direct our attention today to the time between the fourteenth and sixteenth years, accepting that it differs according to climate, nationality, etc. At that time, humans become mature, as we know, and are able to beget children. Now, it will be recognized that the consideration of this particular time is of the greatest importance to the scientific theory of heredity because the human being must by this time have developed all those characteristics that enable him to impart traits to his descendants. He cannot develop these capacities later, so this makes this an important period of life. To be sure, traits of secondary importance that are developed later may be passed over to descendants, but human beings are so constructed from the scientific point of view that they become fully mature between the fourteenth and sixteenth years with respect to transmitting traits to their descendants. It cannot be said, therefore, that what is essential in human development after this point has significance for the question of heredity. Science must find the reasons why humans cease at this point to develop the bases for the transmission of hereditary characteristics. It is entirely different in animals because they make no essential further progress in life beyond this time. It is this that we must carefully consider.

Now, without discussing many related things here, I

120

wish to point out from the spiritual scientific view what really lies at the bottom of the matter. When we fix our attention back beyond the time of birth, a longer period of time stretches out before us that the human being lives through in the spiritual world between the last death and this birth. Within this stretch of time lie those processes I have often described in mere outline. All that takes place then between death and a new birth naturally has an influence on a human being and includes especially many things that are related to what he works out in his physical life between birth and the fourteenth or sixteenth years. The very thing a person is elaborating here mainly in the unconscious, he or she elaborates between death and the new birth from a higher consciousness. Let us be clear about this matter. Here upon the earth the human being perceives through his eyes and other senses the mineral, vegetable, animal world, etc. But while he is in the spiritual world together with Angels, Archangels, Archai, Exusiai, and also with those humans who have passed through the portal of death and are able to be in some close relationship with him, his attention is then directed, when he looks below, primarily upon what is connected with life in this period of time. It is from there, as I have explained even in exoteric lectures, that everything underlying heredity is determined. From a reflection I have already set before you,[83] we know that, as a residue of the processes between death and a new birth, all that results from a previous vocational life manifests itself in the physiognomy, gestures, and in the entire hereditary tendency. Thus, it is really possible to see in the human being during this period of time, in the way he walks, in the movements of his hands, in his general bearing, the result of his vocational life during his previous incarnation.

But then the period from the fourteenth until the twenty-first year begins, which stands in opposition, in a sense, to the preceding period. As you have heard, the hereditary impulses cannot continue to work in the same fashion during this time; the time is past during which these hereditary impulses develop. Science as yet pays no attention whatever to such matters, but, if it is not to be completely divorced from all reality, it will be compelled to do so. This is the period, however, in which the human being is guided toward his new vocation through the vague and unconscious working of certain impulses into which the processes that occur between death and a new birth play in lesser degree. During this period the impulses of the preceding incarnation are effective in far greater measure. While circumstances are thus developing, he believes along with others that he would be impelled to enter this or that vocation even if only these external circumstances were effective. But they are really unconsciously connected with something living within his soul that comes directly from the preceding incarnation. Note the difference. During the preceding period from the seventh to the fourteenth year, the previous incarnation, fructified by what has happened between death and a new birth, passes into our bodily organization, thereby making us a copy of our preceding vocation. In the following period, however, the impulses no longer work into us, no longer impress gestures on us, but guide us on the way to a new vocation.

You will see what infinitely fruitful thought for future education will result from these reflections if only external world culture can decide to reckon with repeated earthly lives, rather than taking fantastic ideas as truths—fantastic because they only consider a fragment of reality, one that encompasses only the present life between birth and death. Here we must gain a perspective of the immeasurable importance of the entrance of spiritual science into those circles connected with the education and development of the human being, and also with the influence on human life of the external social order. Naturally, we are here looking

122

out over wide perspectives, but they are connected through and through with reality; what governs the evolution of the world is not chaos but order—or even disorder, but nevertheless something that is to be explained only on the basis of spiritual life. So a person who knows the laws that are connected with repeated earthly lives can face the world in counsel and deed in an entirely different manner; he can utter things, or even set things in motion, that have to do with the course of human life.

Bear in mind that, after all, everything in the world runs in cycles in a sense. We know, of course, the vast cycles of the post-Atlantean age: the Indian, ancient Persian, Chaldaic-Egyptian, Greco-Latin, our own and what will follow. Human souls are born many times in all these cycles—some of them only once. But it is not only here that we can see how life on earth runs in cycles: it takes its cyclic course in such a way that certain conditions can be determined when one knows how to properly judge previous conditions. If, for instance, we are able to judge in the right way what was spiritually at work in the first centuries of the Christian development—let us say from the third to the seventh centuries—so that we know the spiritual impulses of that time, we can judge, in turn, what social needs may be effective today.

Cyclic evolutions do take place. We bring unhappiness to a person who is destined to be placed in a certain fashion in the cyclic evolution when we advise him or her to assume a different relationship to life. Since, however, human beings must become increasingly conscious in life during our fifth post-Atlantean epoch, a knowledge of the corresponding laws must gradually come to light. It must become possible for a person to consider himself or herself in a connection with what is taking place and playing its role in their environment. This does not consist merely in learning how to direct children to the right vocation, but also in developing the right thoughts—for we know that thoughts are realities—about the relationship one has to the world. No matter what our station in life is, what we may think of all that is occurring in the world due to the development of the spirit of the time will become increasingly important, and the human soul will have to become increasingly more conscious of this.

Now you will recall how I have undertaken to characterize the currents that have arisen with the fifth post-Atlantean epoch. I have shown you[84] how a current has arisen over the western regions that tends especially to make people bourgeois—a comprehensive, approximate expression, but nevertheless the bourgeoisie has arisen in Western Europe and America. We have contrasted this ideal with the pilgrim, the Eastern goal, which is still only a goal since it has come less clearly to expression than that of the comparatively more advanced Western culture. These two ideals, the bourgeois and the pilgrim, face each other and, unless we realize the significance of this for life, we cannot possibly develop the understanding that is growing within us. In earlier ages men could face life without understanding since they were guided by divine spiritual powers; today, however, as we develop toward the future, we must have understanding.

You see, such things as I have explained to you in the form of the two currents, one having its source in heredity and the other in redemption, must be fully considered if we wish to judge life today because they force themselves upon us more and more. That these things press upon us is not a mere assertion of mine but something that may be said from present reality—something felt and to a certain extent known for a long time past by people who were not dull and indolent, but who confronted life with full participation. Indeed, I have already called your attention to the peculiarity of our times. Many people today have a thorough feeling for the things that are coming to pass in life, but they do not possess the ability—remember what I told you about Jaurés[85]—to ascend to an understanding of repeated earthly lives and karma, either of the individual or of the world; they cannot, therefore, comprehend the very thing they perceive. But at numerous points within modern evolution we find those whose eyes are open to what is happening, in spite of the fact that they never developed the ability to explain matters from the standpoint of repeated earthly lives. Because of their failure to accept repeated earthly lives, they contributed much toward bringing about the very conditions they severely criticized. This is exactly the peculiarity of people today, even those of clearest vision; they criticize what exists and yet labor toward bringing about the very things they criticize while judging them correctly. That is how unconscious impulses play into human life.

Let us take, for example, a man who really saw a good deal in an extraordinarily clear manner, especially in the life of his environment. Such was John Stuart Mill,[86] who was born in 1806 and died in 1873, a famous English philosopher, looked upon by many as actually the one who renewed logic and developed it further. He also developed social insights in the most comprehensive way, directing his attention especially to the social evolution of the world as he knew and encountered it in his environment. He wanted to answer the question that assumed for him a tragic character: In what direction does the present age advance? Where does what has forced itself as a social character upon the life of the nineteenth century lead? He said that the bourgeois was the human type that had developed in the nineteenth century and asked how the bourgeois differs from earlier human types. He answered by saying that in earlier times the individual was more significant; that more individuality spoke through the earlier human being. I will couch this more in our concepts, but Mill expressed fundamentally the same thing in his. According to him, the soul had in a certain way elevated itself up above the immediate external physical reality. On the other hand, the bourgeois type works toward levelling and rendering all men equal in the social order. But what, asked Mill, is the result of this process of becoming equal? Not the result of becoming equal in the greatness of the human soul, but of becoming equal in its nothingness. He thus indicates a future for humanity during this fifth post-Atlantean epoch in which men in their social life would become ever more the "pressed caviar" of bourgeois nothingness, and he felt this to be a tragic knowledge.

People sense such things in different ways, however, depending on whether they are born in the Western or Eastern culture. The Russian thinker, Herzen,[87] acquainted himself thoroughly with these assertions, with these items of knowledge presented by Mill. In his soul, however, all this worked differently. The Western thinker describes this perspective of bourgeois life with a certain nonchalance, one might say, but the Eastern thinker suffers terribly under the thought then maintained by Mill and Herzen that Europe was on the way toward taking on the nature of China. As you can deduce from the writing of Herzen of 1864, both Mill and Herzen—the one with an Eastern and the other with a Western coloring—consider what has come about earlier in China as the goal toward which Europe is aiming as a later stage; that is, toward a new Chinese entity in which men will become the "pressed caviar" of bourgeois nullities. A constriction of the intellect will come, says Mill, a constriction of the intellect and of the energies of life, a polishing away of the personality, everything that leads to a levelling down. Constant flattening out of life, as he expresses it, constant exclusion of general human interests from life—so does Mill express the matter, and Herzen confirms it, but from a mood of tragic sensitivity; it is a reduction to the interests of mercantile offices and bourgeois prosperity. So did Mill and Herzen express themselves even in the sixties of the last century! Mill, who speaks first of his own country, said that England was on the way toward becoming a modern China, and Herzen said that not only England but all of Europe was on the way to becoming a modern China. It may be deduced from Herzen's book of 1864 that he and Mill more or less agreed that unless an unexpected upswing should take place in Europe, which might lead to a rebirth of human personality giving it the force needed to overcome the bourgeois, Europe, in spite of its noble forefathers and its Christianity, would become another China. These words were spoken in 1864!

Herzen, however, had no opportunity to take karma and repeated earthly lives into account. He could admit such knowledge as we have mentioned with only the deepest feeling of tragedy, which he expressed by saying that we are not the physicians, but rather the sufferings, of our time because what now approached—perhaps the thought can be better expressed with the English term used by Herzen and Mill than with the German—is "conglomerated mediocrity." Herzen expressed this from a feeling of tragedy, saying that a time will come in Europe when the realism of the modern scientific view will have been carried so far that no one will any longer believe in anything belonging to another, a supersensible, world. It will be said that outward physical realities are the only goal to be striven for, and human beings will be sacrificed for the sake of physical realities without anyone realizing that they are something more than simply the connecting link for those who are to follow. The individual will be sacrificed to the future common colony. Such were the words uttered by Herzen who thought the one barrier to preventing Europe from rapidly becoming another China was Christianity, which is not so easily overcome. Yet, he saw no way of escape. He felt that Christianity had also become shallow, flattened out by revolution, which, as he said, was also growing shallow and had deteri-

127

orated to the bourgeois liberalism of the nineteenth century, to a conglomerated mediocrity. Referring to what Mill had stated and having in mind the downfall of ancient Rome, Herzen said, "I see the inevitable collapse of old Europe; at the portal of the old world (he meant Europe), there stands no Catiline, but death."

With a certain justification and as one who sees much that is around him in the contemporary world yet is utterly unable to admit the sustaining concepts and ideas of spiritual science, the contemporary Russian writer, Merezhkovsky,[88] who has learned a good deal from these two thinkers, Mill and Herzen, remarks that today the yardstick has taken the place of the scepter of earlier times, the account book has usurped the place of the Bible and the sales counter replaces the altar. His mistake lies in not going beyond the mere criticism of these things. The yardstick, the account book, and the counter do have a place in our fifth post-Atlantean epoch. We know that it must be so and that it is in accord with irrevocable world karma. What is needed is not merely to condemn these things, but to pour into this world of the yardstick, the account book, and the counter the spirit that alone is the equal of them; this is the attitude of spiritual science.

These are serious matters, and I wish to make it clear, as I always endeavor to do on such occasions, that I am not merely setting forth what I myself believe, but that what I have expressed is in agreement with those who have viewed life with open and wakeful eyes. Many people may hold views and opinions, but the important question is how these views are related to their time, whether they have roots in the soil of the time and whether these people can prove the things they assert. It is a significant fact that the age is taking on a certain character which can be seen by people who are willing to do so. It is not a question of attributing a certain character to the age in whatever way we please, but that

128

we must really see how the spiritual evolution of humanity
advances from cycle to cycle.

I have called your attention to the fact that there are occult brotherhoods that possess a knowledge of these things
based on traditions handed down from ancient times and
derived from atavistic occult teaching. As you know from
previous discussions, these brotherhoods—especially in the
West but men of the East have also become their adherents
—have taken on a dubious character. This does not prevent
them from preserving certain secrets of existence even
though they do so in a way unsuitable for the present. The
person who listens to the spiritual message for our time and
communicates that portion of spiritual science that can be
given publicly according to the intention of the spirit of the
time, frequently meets with marked opposition that comes
from dark sources. But this opposition is directed and guided
everywhere by spiritual powers, which must always be
taken into consideration. It will readily be understood,
therefore, that today opposition is easily raised against the
spiritual science that is to live within our movement, by the
constantly repeated suggestion that such a spiritual science
should not be created for large groups of people. All sorts of
accepted powers are summoned in order to render this spiritual science innocuous. University professors travel from
one country to another to declare that they are forced to oppose especially *my* spiritual science because people today, as
they say, must look at reality—the kind of reality that they
alone see—and not at such things that draw men away from
it. Often there is method in such attacks because anyone
who is not blind sees how these people seek out the places
that are politically right for them to work most effectively
through the respect felt for them as university professors,
for example; these are the places where they believe they
can most effectually discredit an opponent. They believe
they can accomplish most when they choose the right places

and use the right words; that is, words that speak to current passions.

All these things are contained within a larger relationship, however, and what causes the greatest fear of all, we might even say what horrifies these people, is the thought that a number of individuals might come to understand a little of the characteristic life of our day. The utmost desire is felt, especially by those who belong to the occult brotherhoods I have described, to prevent human beings from attaining clarity in everything connected with the real laws of life, since it is among the uninformed that the interested individual can best work. He can no longer exert an influence when people begin to know how they really stand in the contemporary world. This is dangerous for those who want to fish in troubled waters, who desire to keep their esoteric knowledge to themselves, applying it so as to shape human social relationships as they wish them to be. There are members of occult brotherhoods who, within their own ranks, are fully convinced that spiritual powers are at work everywhere in our environment and that there is a bond between the living and the dead. In fact, within their occult brotherhoods they do not talk about anything except the laws of the spiritual world. Our spiritual science, too, possesses a certain part of this knowledge, but it is soon to be made public. They talk about this truth that they have taken over from ancient atavistic tradition and then publish articles in the newspapers in which they oppose the very same things, branding them as medieval superstitions. These are often the very same persons who, in their secret association, nurture spiritual science as a traditional teaching and then come out in opposition to it in the public press, designating it as a medieval superstition, a traditional mysticism, and so forth. They consider it to be entirely proper that they should not know by what principles they are being guided. Of course, there are also all kinds of strange members of occult brotherhoods who know only as much about the world as

130

they can touch with their noses. They too talk about the present impossibility of imparting publicly the content of mystery teachings to human beings.

Now, there are various ways of keeping human beings in a fog of ignorance as I have indicated in my Liestal lecture[89] and in other public lectures. Just as true spiritual science will impart to us certain ideas and concepts that are like a key giving us access to the spiritual world, so also can certain concepts be found through which it is possible to delude that part of the population that has not arrived at the flattening out of the understanding through a scientific view of the world of which Mill and Herzen speak. Indeed, it is possible to form concepts in more than one way. If it were known how concepts are really formed publicly today in order to manipulate the souls of men in the "right" way, many a person would gradually sense an impulse to come to true spiritual science, which speaks of these things in an honest, upright way. I shall not deal today with all the lofty concepts communicated to persons as ideals, which are not intended, however, to produce what lies within these ideals but rather have an entirely different purpose, but I wish to make clear to you by means of a simple example how those who are craving satisfaction of certain mystical longings are easily deluded.

I will give a most stupid example. It might be said, for instance, that even the ancient Pythagoreans looked upon numbers as containing the laws governing the world. Much is concealed within numerical relationships. Let us take, for example, two numerical relationships:

Nicholas II of Russia:
Born in the year 1868
Ascended the throne in 1894
Reigned for .... 22 years
His age was .... 48 years
Total 3832

Dividing this total by 2, we get 1916, the most important year of the war. This is stated on the basis of a "most secret" numerical relationship. Let us take:

George V of England:
Born in the year	1865
Has reigned since	1910
Has reigned	6 years
His age is	52 years
Total	3832

Half of this is 1916.
The destinies of these two individuals are intimately connected. Here you see how the Pythagorean laws of number play a role in the world! But, to provide a surfeit, let us take also:

Poincaré:
Born in the year	1860
Has ruled since	1913
That amounts to	3 years
His age is	56 years
Total	3832

Half of this is 1916.
You see how the numbers agree among these three Allies!

It is, of course, one of the dumbest examples imaginable. If I now went down into the audience and asked one of the ladies—as I shall naturally not do—when she was born, how long she has been a member of the Anthroposophical Society, how old she is—which, as I have said, I shall not ask—when she became a member of the Society, and then added these numbers and took half of the total, I would arrive at precisely the same figure. It is an ideal example and so that it may include present reality, let us select, then, any lady or gentlemen; it may just as well be a gentlemen:

XY was born in the year	1870
He entered the Anthroposophical Society	1912
So he was in the Society	4 years
And he is	46 years old
Total	3832

Half of this is 1916.

It is a really absurd example. I can assure you, however, that all sorts of things that have to do with searching out the secrets of numbers rest on nothing more; the problems are simply a little more concealed than those I have given. Moreover, concepts taken from other fields can just as well be shaped in the right manner and used for throwing dust into the eyes of people; by using proper methods people are hindered from seeing what is concealed behind these things and many have been taken in even by the example I have given. It is profoundly significant that destiny chooses 1916. Had we calculated for 1914, it would have been connected with the beginning of the war! Just as these numbers have been put together for these three Allies, any kind of numbers can, after all, be put together. Many things have been similarly fabricated from different concepts but they are not at all more significant or intelligent. They are less easily observed when somewhat more concealed. Then, when all sorts of numerical relationships are produced along with such expressions as "unfathomable," and "deep as the world," anyone can find innumerable adherents and also give the impression that he is speaking from profound depths of human knowledge. But there is really something to the methods used by certain individuals who wish to throw dust in the eyes of the people. In one place or another this or that concept is made public and other things are added, and those pronouncements go back to some occult connection which calls for the attainment of certain purposes. Then one must only become acquainted with the course these people will adopt.

If such things are to become impossible in the future, it is necessary that a number of people shall not have that constricted understanding and energy of life to which Mill refers; rather, they must have the sustaining understanding and supporting life energy that come from spiritual science. These are to work in a fructifying way upon the intellect and life energy of men so that their approach to life shall be such that no one can delude them. These things are connected with the feeling of fear and even horror which the strange news—travelling from eastern Europe to the West—aroused that an individual such as Mme. Blavatsky[90] had made her appearance as if coming from nowhere. I have often pointed out[91] that this was decidedly significant for the course of the nineteenth century. She appeared at the very time when the struggle was most bitter between the so-called esotericists and the so-called progressive occultists. That is, the reactionaries called themselves the esotericists. They used the word thus because they wished to keep the occult secrets to themselves. The life of Blavatsky fell into this period. There was the danger, through the special construction of this life in which truly far-reaching forces were at work from the subconscious, that spiritual secrets might be revealed through her and people might learn something in the right way. This danger really existed and people were living under it from the 1840's on—in a sense, ever since her birth or childhood. From then on, there was a constant endeavor so to arrange things that Blavatsky might be brought into the service of the Western occult brotherhoods. She would then have been able to bring to light only what they considered suitable for their own ends.

The whole affair took a strange turn, however. I have told you how the effort was made at first by the "Grand Orient" to lure Blavatsky, and how this failed because she set conditions that could not be fulfilled. She then caused mischief in an American brotherhood because her temperament always rebelled against what others wanted to do with her. I have told you how she was then expelled, and how there was no way left to deal with her other than by imposing upon her a kind of occult imprisonment, and by bringing her into the Indian occult brotherhood, whose practice of occultism was considered harmless to the so-called Western brotherhoods because it resembled that of Blavatsky. They thought, "Oh well, even if all sorts of things come to light from Indian sources, they are by no means able to disturb our circles much." Most of the occultists who were working with serious occultism said, "Now, how can anything much result since we have surrounded Blavatsky with all those pictures that shut her out from a real knowledge of the spiritual world. She will take in only such things as the old ladies, male and female, discuss among themselves at afternoon teas (I am quoting here!) and this will not seriously disturb our circles."

The affair became uncomfortable only after *our* movement appeared, which took things in a serious way and opened an access to the fountainhead of a real spiritual world. But you also see that the bases of the conflicts that then resulted lie most deep. The truth is that something of the impulses that had to come from the Eastern world actually was in Blavatsky, and there was really a certain necessity for a synthesis to take place with the Western World. But the important fact was that it had gradually come about that certain purposes and goals were striven for which, as I have already indicated, do not have truth as their objective but are really seeking quite different goals. Think about it, when it is known how human cycles take their course and what the character of the present world must be in relation to its Archai after this or that has happened in earlier evolution, it is then possible to be active in accordance with this truth. If a person possesses, on the one hand, traditional occult knowledge and, on the other, comes out in the press and public life against this occult knowledge as a medieval superstition, he can work in the dark and achieve the important things he is actually striving for. Things are interrelated in the world, but it is not always necessary that people should understand what the interrelationships are, because for many these connections can play their role in the subconscious. As I have indicated yesterday, what is important is that one knows how to direct one's perception to the right places. There something often appears to be quite insignificant, but when seen in the right connection, it explains much more than is explained by what one considers to be significant. Here the same thing may be said regarding many other things in the world, as Hamlet asserted concerning good and evil: Nothing is good or evil in itself, but man makes it so in his thoughts. So it is also with many other matters. The significance of one thing or another is not to be found in what it represents for outer maya, for the great illusion, but the significance of things must be recognized by associating the right concepts with them. I will mention an example taken from the most recent times in Europe, without thereby intending to enter any sort of partisan or political current.

There may be men here in Europe who, since they all like to think short-sightedly nowadays, look upon the outbreak of the present war as being connected with the murder of the Archduke Franz Ferdinand,[92] Heir Apparent to the Throne. I do not say that this is untrue or that there is no truth in it, but on the basis of this event they can explain certain occurrences that they trace back to this murder of

136

July 1914. But there may also be other persons who stress that, in a Western newspaper of January 1913, the statement appeared that the Archduke Franz Ferdinand was to be murdered in the near future for the well-being of European humanity. What I mean to say is that we may go back as far as the actual murder, but we may also go back to the notice of it that appeared in a Western newspaper in January 1913.[93] It is also possible to go back to the murder of Jaures on the last evening before the war began—probably never entirely explained, as I recently suggested. But it is equally possible to go back to the same newspaper to which I just referred, which carried the statement in 1913 saying that if conditions in Europe should lead to war, Jaures would be the first to meet his death—You may consult a certain occult almanac[94] that was sold for forty francs and find in the issue for 1913, which was printed, of course, in 1912, the statement that he who was expected to be the ruler in Austria would not be the ruler, but rather a younger man, whom people wouldn't even now consider as the successor to the old Emperor Franz Josef.[95] That was printed in a so-called occult almanac for 1913; printed, therefore, in the autumn of 1912. Moreover, in the same almanac for 1914, printed in 1913, the same remark was repeated[96] because obviously the attempt on Emperor Franz Josef's life had miscarried in 1913. When these things are seen more clearly, the connection will someday be discovered that exists between what actually happens externally and what is cooked up by hidden, dark sources. Many will recognize the threads that lead from public life into this or that brotherhood, and how stupid it is for other brotherhoods continually to declare that silence should be maintained regarding certain mystery truths. Such people may be as innocent as children, in spite of the fact that they may be old members of this or that brotherhood of Freemasons which lay claim

137

to secret sources. Nevertheless, they further intensify the obscurity and darkness that is already present among human beings.

I recently gave an example in St. Gallen and Zurich of an especially enlightened pastor and professor, [97] who belongs to an occult brotherhood, and pointed out the discontinuity in his thinking. He is one of those people who make their presence felt through their own denseness which they acquire in their occult brotherhoods. It is the mission of many leaders in those brotherhoods to keep members like this professor in the dark, and by this a rather unfavorable influence is exerted. People must open their eyes, but these eyes must first learn how to see. The direction of one's perception is determined by the enlightenment one has received regarding the spiritual world. Judgments are continually made that seldom take human relationships into account. Thus, as I have once indicated, I, too, was at one time to be made tractable through being "appointed" to some post in the Theosophical Society at the time Alcyone (Krishnamurti)[98] was "appointed." Everything that pulses through our movement might have been neatly swept away if I had fallen in with what was suggested to me; that is, to become the "reincarnated John"! Certain sources would then have announced that Alcyone is one thing and *he* is the reincarnated John. Then the entire movement need not have experienced what later occurred.

Vanity also belongs among the various things that stupefy people. Much can be achieved by getting hold of it in the right way, especially if the methods are known by which certain concepts are to be formed. I have already pointed out that the Theosophical Society simply worked too amateurishly. The others do these things more cleverly and practically, but it is naturally not possible to do much that is clever when it is necessary to reckon with a personality under whom those near her have groaned a good deal;

when it is necessary, for example, to reckon with such a personality as Annie Besant,[99] who is full of violent emotion. Those in her company have sighed for years because of the state into which they declared she would bring them because she also, of course, had come within the aura of a particular Indian occultism. Moreover, she also possessed curious characteristics that came from strange depths and were rather inappropriate for a number of people even in the Theosophical Society. A number of individuals, mostly men—excuse me, but no allusion is intended—groaned because they were forever trying to get Annie Besant a little more on the track so things might proceed. But there were women also who sighed, and they always gave in to her again since they always tried, above all, to practice theosophy —to be sure, in the sense in which it was there practiced, but in such a way that it should become something like a theosophical sort of conglomerated mediocrity. There was a desire to introduce into the practice of spiritual science what John Stuart Mill called conglomerated mediocrity.

I myself observed how a representative of the Theosophical Society worked in a city belonging to the section of which I was at that time the general secretary.[100] I went to this city to deliver some lectures, having been called there by a lady representative. But she said to me, "We shall gradually give up the lectures because they do not have the right objective. We must arrange afternoon teas and invite people to become mutually acquainted." Her idea was that this is done best along with sandwiches. "But the lectures (and she said this with a certain disparaging expression) will have a less and less important role." It may be said that this personality was also enveloped in the right sheaths from a particular direction. There are, indeed, many individuals working as representatives who do not know at times where the wires that pull them originate. Wires are frequently not needed. Small twine will work, even packaging cord. Indeed, it is lamentable to see how humanity behaves at times even when the holiest and most serious things of mankind are at stake.

In particular, the greatest fear was that Blavatsky, provided she continued to be healthy and brought up to the surface what was in the subconscious parts of her nature, would be politically dangerous simply because of her special gifts and exceptional connection with her own Russian people. Many special efforts were made to prevent this from happening. Indeed, beginning in the sixties and seventies, if what then lived in Blavatsky could have become effective, many things of which such individuals as Mill and Herzen had a perfectly clear view would then have taken an entirely different course. But certain ahrimanic powers succeeded in eliminating a great deal. Well, we will see how things will go with our spiritual science under the present distressing conditions. Right thinking about it will be possible only for those who are capable of perceiving its significance in reference to the mission of our fifth post-Atlantean epoch. You have already been able to discover to what extent our spiritual science really takes into account only what is purely human, and I think it is also possible to perceive a distinction between these things. We have often discussed Goethe's *Faust* and even produced it on the stage. It does not require a national background to present *Faust* in all its occult depths. But I leave it up to you to decide whether it is necessary to harbor nationalistic feelings or perhaps even a peculiar nationalistic fervor, in order to call Goethe, Schiller, and Lessing spirits of mediocre rank, as Maeterlinck[101] has most recently done, and to write long articles about the mediocrity of Goethe, Schiller, and Lessing that the important newspapers of the world are persuaded to publish. You may decide there are even deeper reasons behind this.

Just put two things together. In the course of these reflections I have pointed out to you that Ku Hung-Ming,[102] the Chinese, has written a truly ingenious book claiming that the only salvation for the Europeans is to apply themselves to what is the essence of China. Thus, they would be enabled, so Ku Hung Ming thinks, to replace their worthless Magna Carta of freedom[103] with a Magna Carta of loyalty, which can come only from what is essentially Chinese. Ku Hung Ming is a discerning spirit who, from a profound knowledge of the Chinese nature, confirms what Mill and Herzen already had sensed. He is a spirit, moreover, who is not a philologist or schoolmaster, but one who came from a practical profession like Max Eyth, whom I have already mentioned; that is, he is neither a theologian, schoolmaster nor philologist, but one who originally was a merchant, has had many occupations and knows life. Ku Hung Ming represents the Chinese nature, the life of China. From Ku Hung Ming's remarkably vivid descriptions, it is possible today to gain a conception that gives us the impression that Mill and Herzen—read Herzen's book of 1864—were entirely right when they called the teaching of Confucius and Laotze[104] the final consequence that must follow if Europe should be seized by the so-called positivistic realism, supported by conglomerated mediocrity, by bourgeois nothingness. The Chinese way of thinking is the final consequence of what is promulgated in the universities today and is spreading to the masses as the contemporary world view. It came from an earlier culture six hundred years before our era. Ku Hung Ming describes it clearly. Mill and Herzen described the way that will be taken by a European culture based solely upon external positivistic realism. From one side Europe will take hold of the Chinese entity; from the other, the only salvation for Europe lies in the Chinese way of thinking.

Perhaps there may be a third side and I hope you will permit me to raise this very question at the conclusion of today's considerations. How would it be if there were also a side to which it would be entirely agreeable if a Chinese should advise the Europeans to choose their only existing salvation? How would it be if it were not mere chance that this teaching of Ku Hung Ming is being introduced into Europe today? It is brilliant from the standpoint of the Chinese nature, but is it not also capable of confusing those people who do not receive it with a clear mind, with senses awakened by spiritual science and possibly designed to maneuver the people to a point where they embrace the ways of China? This is precisely what is intended, just as Mill and Herzen have already correctly seen that certain occult brotherhoods have set their sails in the direction of acquiring the essence of China, since in a Chinafied Europe it would be easiest to include what they want. Why, then, should it not be in keeping with the will of a brotherhood that a Chinese should advise the Europeans to pay heed to the beauties that might come from this Chinese way of thinking? Why may we not expect that the so-called most enlightened should be captivated by the advice of a Chinese since Europeans no longer know what to do?

Since I have said how significant that Chinese book is, I also feel obligated from the representative standpoint of spiritual science to call attention to the following: Such phenomena as the book of Ku Hung Ming—or really, the books, since two have appeared—should certainly be examined but we also must know that, under certain circumstances, far-reaching objectives are concealed behind them. It is entirely wrong not to become acquainted with them, but it is also wrong to be taken in by them. It is also most important to examine carefully everything that appears today, often from the most dubious sources, in the form of mysticism or occultism. Those of you who take into account what I have so frequently presented will endeavor also to see these things correctly. The modern world stands in the midst of all sorts of other currents, raising the question as to

142

whether or not individuals possess the will power to see clearly and distinctly. We must, for example, be able to estimate thoroughly the difference between this current and one that still possesses more power today than is ordinarily supposed, and that proceeds from certain Roman Catholic sources. Initiation principles frequently stand behind them, though naturally those who bring them into the world are blind to what guides them. Let us now contrast certain things with others. On the one side, there is the Roman Church and, on the other, those occult brotherhoods. The Roman Church, which works in the way well-known to you, and those brotherhoods that, of course, wage a deadly war with the Church but also certainly possess and use occult knowledge; yet, before the public, they brand this as medieval superstition so that they may keep people in the right current and use them for their own purposes. Contrast this with the Roman Church. Just take the encyclical of December 8, 1864, *Freedom of Conscience and of Worship*,[105] that was proclaimed *ex cathedra*. Those principles in which men believe are mentioned there and they are then condemned: "It is stated by some people that freedom of conscience and or worship is the right of every human being. This is madness. This is an absurdity." In the view of the Roman See, it is an absurdity, a madness, for the orthodox Catholic to lay claim to freedom of conscience and worship. This is one of the currents; the other finds that it is better not to say such things but rather to do things whereby the freedom of conscience, the freedom of one's own conviction, most of all, and the introduction of one's own conviction in human life, shall be abolished. Here you have two contrasting movements that are most significant for today; much depends on this.

The reason for my concluding today's lecture with these reflections was to admonish those who stand within our spiritual scientific movement to grasp the inner impulse of the soul and not belong among the somnolent, but among those who determine to strive for a vision of life as it is. To receive items of spiritual scientific knowledge and to believe them does not make one a spiritual scientist. Only that person is a spiritual scientist in the true sense whom the spiritual scientific truths have made into a clear-sighted human being, but also into one who possesses the will really to look in the right way at what is in his other environment, and at the right points, so as to be able to judge the situation in which one is placed in the world. If we wish to speak in a fruitful way about the karma of vocation, then this also belongs to the discussion.

We shall soon continue these reflections. The necessary light will then be cast upon what belongs more in the immediate, everyday life, the immediate karma of vocation.

VIII

Our present considerations will impress us with their deeper and real meaning only if we do not take them in a merely theoretical way, since they are in the highest sense truths of life. Rather, we must draw from them certain consequences for our feelings and sentiments that may enable us to look upon life differently than is often done by those who have not been prepared to do so by an anthroposophical view. Our minds must be broadened through spiritual science to grasp the truth of life. This means that we must learn to compare the nature of truth as it meets us in life with the one-sided thinking about the truth that so easily befalls people. It is all too easy to get into the habit of forming opinions about this or that, not merely about everyday matters but also about the most important facts of life, and then fortifying our point of view with this opinion, paying no attention to the fact that the world may be viewed from the most varied standpoints. Thus, we can attain to the truth only when we feel and realize how everything, every single fact, can be viewed from many standpoints. I will relate the course of a certain life in order that I may give you an example, a kind of illustration of what I mean. We are now dealing with what we call karma, the passage of the human being through repeated earthly lives, the destiny of man, which is expressed in the course a human life takes. We can learn much through the examples of individual lives if we view them correctly in the light of repeated earthly lives.

In this example, we have to do with a person who was

born in the sixteenth century. In order to consider the hereditary influences that people today like to emphasize, let us first look at his father. The father of this man who was born in the sixteenth century was a rather versatile person but also an extraordinarily obstinate one; this was characterized by a certain harshness in the expression of his life. He was well-acquainted with music, played the lute and other string instruments, was also familiar with geometry and mathematics, and his profession was that of a merchant. His harshness may be more readily understandable from the following. He had a certain music teacher who, at that time in the sixteenth century, was a highly respected man. As a pupil of this man, he wrote a book on music, but this did not please his teacher and he took issue with it in a book of his own. The pupil then became really quite angry and wrote another volume in which he included all possible contempt he could muster against the "ancient and rusty views" of his music teacher. Then he dedicated the book to him, saying expressly in the dedication, "Since you deigned to turn against me in such an obtrusive manner, I want to give you an opportunity to experience this pleasure more often. You obviously enjoy this sort of thing and that is why I dedicate this book to you."

The son of this man is the person whose course of life I wish to tell you about in a slightly disguised way. As was the custom in those days, he at first pursued the study of Greek and Latin with a famous teacher in Italy because his father attached great importance to having him well-instructed. He studied the humanities with a monk, learned mathematics from his father and, in addition, learned drawing, perspective, and the like with other teachers. Possessing an extraordinary capacity for mathematics and mechanics, he continued to excel in these fields and became quite a versatile young man. Even as a boy he had made all sorts of models of machines that were useful at that time. Today, you know, boys make only airplanes, but then other ships were made. At eighteen, the young man went to the university, studying medicine at first—excuse this just after we have heard that passage from *Faust*.[106] But he had a somewhat different experience than the student who has just been presented to you in that scene of "Mephisto and the Student." He did not pass through his medical studies as if he were in a dream, nor did he say, "They're not so bad." No, he really disliked studying medicine since he found that this discipline proceeded in an unsystematic way, one fact simply following after another with no true connection. Then he turned to philosophy. In those days it was the custom of some individuals to attack Aristotle, the Greek philosopher who had hitherto been so greatly honored. Having one of these critics as his teacher, our young man fell into the same habit of criticizing and hating Aristotle. Although his father was an extraordinarily competent man, he was not well-liked because of his various characteristics. So, after his son had studied for a few years, he did not have much money and tried to secure a scholarship for him. He did not succeed, however, and was compelled to provide further instruction for him with the money he earned with sweat and blood.

After the son had struggled through his medical and philosophical studies, he had reason to feel most fortunate. He became a professor at one of the most famous universities of his country, teaching mathematics and also practicing medicine, of which he had a good deal of knowledge from his student days. On the whole, he was a quite popular teacher. But at this university things got a little hot for him. This came about through a book that was published containing a description of a public project, a mechanical project. It was written by an eminent gentleman who was not too intelligent, but who was the son of an actual princely personality of that particular state. Our professor, although

147

still relatively young, had little difficulty in proving it would be impossible to carry out this project. Much hostility was then aroused against him and, although he had already succeeded in attracting attention to himself through his accomplishments, he no longer felt entirely comfortable in that particular city and university. The opportunity arose to go to another university in a republical state. At this university also, he soon became well-known, had many students and, what was then a mere matter of course, gave many private lessons so that he had an excellent income. He needed a good deal of money because his father had died and he had to support his mother and sisters. In order that we may see a little more clearly into the karma of this person let me mention the following authenticated fact; it was related by a contemporary to whom it was told by the man himself. Moreover, no matter with what philological finesse the endeavor is made to get at the fact, it is demonstrably true. This man with whom we are dealing, now teaching in a republican university, once had a dream in which he saw himself walking over burning coals and ashes and knew that they must have come from the burning of the cathedral in the city where he had previously been a professor. He related this dream and also wrote of it in many letters. It was later revealed that the very same night he had this dream, the cathedral had actually burned down.

Now, he was most successful; indeed, he made significant scientific discoveries, for which others claimed part of the credit as was then the custom and is still so to some extent even now, without thanking him. He became fairly prosperous but not sufficiently so in his own mind, especially since he had to drive himself so hard. He had to give many private lessons, earning a little thereby, to be sure, but it required a good deal of work. Now, his Italian contemporaries and later others tell in an interesting way how he was a man so much occupied with his brain that—I simply repeat what was related—he had little time to pay attention to the impulses of his heart. He was, therefore, quite clever but somewhat less lovable. Thus, he never officially married but lived, as his contemporaries say, in a common-law marriage with a certain Marina Gamba by whom he had two daughters, whom he sent into a convent, and a son, whom he later legitimized. Although he became the instructor of many famous people—for example, he taught Gustav Adolf, who later became the king of Sweden—things were not entirely as he wished them. So he applied to the Grand Duke of his native land where he had previously been a professor. This was in 1610. The fact was that he was striving to gain more free time to devote to inventions and discoveries. It is interesting, therefore, to observe the man somewhat more carefully since he was really a sort of child of his age. For this reason I should like to read to you, in a pretty good translation, a letter that he wrote to obtain a more fitting position at the court of the Grand Duke. He writes to a friend about his correspondence with the Grand Duke:

Your grace's letter was heartily welcome, first, because it lets me know that his most serene Highness, the Grand Duke, my Lord, remembers me, and then because it assures me of the continued goodwill of the right honorable Signor Aeneas Piccolomini, infinitely highly treasured by me, as also of the love of your Grace, which causes you to perceive my interest and induces you to write me in such friendly fashion about circumstances of great importance. For this service I remain always under obligation both to the right honorable Signor Aeneas and also to your Grace, render you endless thanks, and consider it my duty, as evidence of the value I attach to such goodness, to speak with these gentlemen concerning thoughts and those life relationships in which it would be my desire to pass

149

the years that still remain to me. I hope that an opportunity might present itself when the right honorable Aeneas, with his keenness and versatility, might give a more definite answer to our august Lord, toward whose Highness, in addition to that reverent relationship and most obedient subjection that is due him from every one of his loyal servants, I feel myself, moreover, inclined with such special devotion and, as I may be permitted to say, so much love. Even God does not require any other feeling of us than that we should love Him, but I would set aside every other interest, and there is no position whatever for which I would not exchange my own state if I should learn that this would please His Highness. This answer might then suffice to realize any decision it might please His Highness to form in regard to my person. But if, as we may assume, His Highness, full of humanity and goodness, which renders him worthy of fame among all others and will ever render him more and more worthy, will unite together with my service to him every other satisfaction for me, I will then not refrain from speaking my mind. For twenty years now, and indeed throughout the best part of my life, I have labored even to minute detail, as it is said, upon the demand of anybody and everybody, to share any small talent that had come into my possession from God or through my own endeavors in my vocation. But now I would really wish to attain sufficient leisure and peace to be able to bring to completion before my life ends three great works I have on my hands so that I may publish these. I would hope to do this perhaps to the honor of myself and also of everyone who might support me in such undertakings, through the fact that I would perhaps bring to those studying in this special field greater, more general, and more lasting service than I could otherwise do for the rest of my life. I do not believe that I could have greater leisure elsewhere than I have here as long as I am compelled to obtain the support of my family out of my official duties as a teacher and from private lessons. Moreover, I would not willingly do such work in another city than in this one, for various reasons that it would be too cumbersome to enumerate. Yet, the freedom I have here is not sufficient, since I must sacrifice, upon the demand of one person and another, many hours of the day and often the best. No matter how brilliant and generous a republic, to retain a remuneration from it without rendering service to its general community is not customary. As long as I am able to give lectures and to render service, no one in a republic can release me from this obligation without ending my income; in short, I cannot hope to receive such a favor from anyone else than an absolute prince. Yet I should not wish, after what I have said, to appear to make unjustified claims upon your Grace, as if I were seeking for support without a corresponding service and obligation. That is not my purpose; on the contrary. As concerns a corresponding service, I have various inventions of which even a single one would suffice to provide a support for my life, if I should meet a great prince who should take pleasure in it. Experience shows me that things that are, perhaps, of far less significant value have a great advantage for their discoverer, and it had always been my thought to place these things before my Prince and natural master rather than before others. He in turn could do with these things and with the inventor as he might see it, and to receive from them, if it should please him, not only the ore, but also the metal. I find new things of this kind every day and would find many more if I had the leisure and more favorable opportunities to secure skillful persons whose help I could utilize in various investigations. So far as concerns further the daily rendering of service—that is, public and private lectures—I have only a distaste against that venal servitude in which I must offer my work in exchange for whatever remuneration pleases any purchaser; but to render service to a Prince or a great Lord, and to anyone dependent upon him, would never cause me any feeling of repugnance. On the contrary, I would earnestly desire this and strive for it, and since your Grace wanted to know from me something about my income here, I will tell you that the compensation for my service amounts to 520 gold gulden, which will be changed to an equal number of scudi within a few months when I receive my new position, of which I am just as good as certain. This money I can in great part save, since I obtain a large supplementary assistance for the support of my household through having private students and through my earnings from private lessons, although I rather discourage than seek to give many such lessons. I have a far greater longing for more free time than for money, since I know that it would be much more difficult for me to acquire a sufficient sum of money to give me any distinction than a certain amount of fame through my scientific work.

This man was then really summoned to this court. The only requirement was that he deliver lectures on the occasions when there were unusual events, brilliant occasions, festival affairs at which the Grand Duke had to appear and where it was necessary to make a good impression on foreign visitors. As for the rest, he was simply to receive his support salary and devote himself entirely to his studies. For a time things went well, indeed. Even poets, noblemen, and princes honored him and held all kinds of festivities because they considered him a great man. He himself—it was on February 3, 1613—composed the text for a masquerade in which he represented himself as Jupiter enthroned on the clouds. He could easily be recognized in his disguise and since the four moons of Jupiter had just been discovered by Galileo[107] and had been given the names of the four princes of the house, even these four princes appeared in the entourage. It was an altogether unusual, festive pageantry.

The kindness of the Prince, however, gradually subsided and after a certain time he actually betrayed this man of learning. The clergy found that his views did not agree with theirs. Moreover, he was impoverished at the close of his life and died in genuine disillusionment. He had thoroughly tasted the ingratitude and fickleness of fate. He had learned fully how some princes behave in the long run, and he had experienced the hatred of the clergy.

I have now given you a factual account of the life of a human being. But now I would like to relate this life story in a different way, from another perspective, as it were.

On February 18, 1564, the great Galileo was born. His father, Vincenzo Galileo, was extraordinarily well-acquainted with music, played the lute and other string instruments well, was occupied with geometry, and at first taught his son music himself. The boy pursued his studies in Latin and Greek with distinguished teachers; he learned the humanities with a monk and then went to the University of Pisa where he studied medicine without much satisfaction, then turned to philosophy, became an anti-Aristotelian under the influence of the contemporary anti-Aristotelian tendency. At that time he was already such a genius that one day as he sat in the Cathedral of Pisa watching the church lamp swing, he discovered the principle of the pendulum's isochronism, a most important discovery that has had significance ever since. This event was told by Galileo's contemporaries. I am constantly being told that this story is a myth, but I will continue to relate it because it is true.

In spite of the importance of Galileo's thoughts upon observing this swinging church lamp, his father could not obtain a stipend for him. Then, after he had pursued his geometrical studies, he became a professor at the University of Pisa. There he lectured on mathematics for sixty scudi a year and also practiced medicine. We know that he actually did practice medicine from a letter he wrote to his father in which he asked that the writings of the ancient physician Galen be sent him as a guide. He sharply criticized the writing of the highly placed but imprudent Cosimo I[108] that was published at that time. Then things became too hot for him in Pisa and since the Venetian Republic invited him to teach there, appreciating him more than his native state, he went to Padua in 1592. Galileo Galilei became a professor at the University of Padua and lectured with great distinction on mathematics and related subjects; he also constructed sun dials according to special principles and perfected the knowledge of mechanics. It was there that Giambattista Doni in his letters on dreams wrote that Galileo had the dream of which I have told you; this was the dream where he was walking over glowing coals and ashes. The Cathedral of Pisa burned at the time Galileo had his dream, and he wrote of this in letters to many contemporaries. About this time he invented the proportional circles and machines for raising water, made important discoveries in connection with the telescope and the thermoscope, and made observations regarding the barometer and other things, credit for which was claimed by other people, whereas in most cases it is to be attributed to him. I have already told you the story of his common-law marriage; it happened as I related it so I need not repeat it. Likewise, his letter was written in the way I have told you. Thus, he was actually transferred from

Padua back to his native state and things happened to him there as I have said. It was Galileo who produced that masquerade in which he represented himself as Jupiter enthroned on the clouds, and it was he who gave the names of the Medici to the four satellites of Jupiter, which led to their representing them at this festival. The fact that he was not well-treated by the clergy, and that, in relation to it, he was betrayed by his prince, is known from history. Although all sorts of things in the story of his recantation are true, the assertion made by everybody that he said, "And yet it does move," is certainly false. I have frequently pointed this out.

So this is the matter when it is reenacted from another point of view. You will observe that even though I did not relate false things the first time, your feelings for the man were probably not the same as when I related the story the second time. And you will also agree that your feelings the second time were definitely those that almost every person has when he or she thinks about Galileo, the astronomer. You will see from this that much knowledge is lacking in what many think. They certainly do not know much about Galileo but think and feel about him, not because of what they know, but because the name Galileo Galilei has a certain significance in history.

We must take into consideration, however, that what a man produces through his genius has meaning for the physical world. The fact that there are satellites around Jupiter was a discovery of immense importance for the evolution of the earth, but it has no significance for the concerns of the spiritual world, that is, for the beings of the higher hierarchies. So it is with the other discoveries of Galileo. They are such that they have a great significance for the earth. What, then, was the substance of what I first related? It was his personal fate. Apart from the fact that Galileo was an important man because of his earthly discoveries, it was his personal fate, the misery he experienced in his vocation,

155

his—well, what shall I say—perhaps his loyalty toward the Prince, and so forth. In other words, I first told you what his daily affairs were, but because it concerns him personally it is also what has significance when he bears it through the portal of death and has to develop it between death and a new birth. We must go into such studies as this to educate ourselves regarding the question of human destiny, which cuts so deeply into life. It is precisely with significant, distinguished human lives that we must do this.

There is much talk about heredity nowadays and many questions are considered solely in connection with it. I first told you the story of the life of Galileo in such a way that you could observe it without any preconception. I related his life to that of his father, so that we perhaps might again have an example of right thinking about the question of heredity. It is certainly impossible to think correctly of it without taking into consideration the teaching of repeated earthly lives. In such a thought process, heredity does not prove to be without meaning, but is, on the contrary, most meaningful. There also appears, however, the connection between the inherited characteristics and what the human being brings down from the spiritual world through his own individuality as a result of his previous earthly life. When we wish to decide what is really inherited, we simply have to look at the facts of life.

On a previous occasion I called your attention to the fact that the period of puberty is not taken into consideration at all by science today, whereas it should be when heredity is discussed. Up to this period a person must carry with him all the impulses of heredity. What comes later must be referred to another point of time. I mentioned this a week ago. But what, then, really is inherited? The unprejudiced observation of the following facts is testimony for the arbitrary manner in which scientists interpret things in this field, but they are utterly incapable of understanding them. Since it is known to anybody who can observe life, it must be known to every psychiatrist that there may be two sons in a family who have the same inherited potentialities. Let us define the two sets of hereditary potentialities that may be similar. First, there is a certain tendency to think out concepts and connections and to apply them to external life; second, there is a certain—what shall we call it?—peppy or fashionable bearing such as a businessman must have. Once there were two sons who both had these traits; that is, a certain self-consciousness and from it a certain boldness in bringing to realization what occurred to them. These were simply inherited characteristics, and it is thus that they must, in general, be conceived. But the question now is: What did each of them become? What course did their karmas take? One of them became a poet whose achievements were pretty respectable. The other became a swindler. The inherited characteristics were applicable to both activities; in one individual, they could be applied to the art of poetry, and in the other, to all kinds of swindles. Whatever comes from physical life was similar in these brothers. These things must really be studied conscientiously and earnestly and not in the way contemporary science often studies them. Indeed, we often find that the people themselves register the facts quite correctly nowadays, but they cannot make anything of them because they do not possess the ability to connect them with the great law of repeated earthly lives.

Influenced by the currents of our time, people in a few regions have begun to think of how it may be possible to assist nature according to the physical line of heredity, the stream of heredity, as the materialist says—they do not say Divine Providence. The brilliant minds of many individuals are especially impelled to reflect on how offspring may be produced in our sad time. But in the minds of most people, this question is identical with that of how families may be assisted to have as many children as possible; that is, how the conditions conducive to producing the greatest number of descendants may be established scientifically. One who can see through things can readily foresee what will come about. Those who are displaying their scientific theories about the best possible conditions for producing future progeny will be completely fooled simply because they refuse to learn anything. All they would have to do would be to observe the results in instances where excellent conditions existed for the production of children. For example, there is the case of the well-known Johann Sebastian Bach,[109] who was cantor in the Thomas School in Leipzig some two hundred years ago, and who played a great deal of music with his ten musical sons. No one can say that this family with ten sons was unfruitful. But you can go all the way back to the great grandfather of Johann Sebastian Bach. He also had sons. There were so many sons throughout the generations that almost the entire family was as prolific as Johann Sebastian himself. That is to say that what constitutes favorable conditions for having descendants was present in this family in the most eminent sense. Nevertheless, by 1850, a hundred years after the death of Johann Sebastian Bach, the entire family had died out; not a single descendant was left. There you have what needs to be studied. Thus, when people with their new method will have come up with their so-called favorable conditions, they will not be able to prevent the possible generation of ten-member families, but after fifty years such families may no longer exist.

We shall speak again tomorrow of how conditions arise under which humanity evolves and how these are quite different from those at which our natural philosophic world conception labors with its utter lack of all wisdom. But this scientific world conception is simply one of the outcroppings of materialism. I have already told you that those who are familiar with the fundamental laws of the occult conception of the world knew that in the middle of the nineteenth century we reached the lowest point—or, as the materialists might designate it, the highest point—of materialistic thinking, feeling, and willing. We have already learned to know much that is connected with this materialistic thinking, and we shall still have to learn much more. But what strikes us time and again is the fact that even well-meaning persons are by no means inclined to become acquainted with the materialistic impulses dominating the depths and heights regarding human perception and will. Here people are really astonishingly little inclined to submit to what has so often been discussed, that is, to seeing the world with open eyes. What will become of the world if the views that have spread over the entire earth in the second half of the nineteenth century continue to develop further? In the course of these lectures we shall have to speak about the deep inner reasons for these things in our time.

We must, however, confront our souls with the question of how far things have really gone in some fields. Indeed, the nineteenth century was the period in which the view was presented that a real scientist could not possibly accept the childish and absurd conceptions of the ancient religions. What has been preserved in them—and we shall later discuss how it has been preserved—was considered mere childishness. It was considered the mark of an enlightened person to have risen above the assumption of a spiritual-psychic organism in the human being and that he is to be especially distinguished from animals. Not only was the endeavor made to establish a physical connection between human beings and animals, but the endeavor was also made to prove that they are nothing but animals, that is, simply a little different from other animals just as other animals differ from one another. That is the very point these people wanted to make, and it was from this point of view that not only natural histories were written, but also psychological texts. Pick up at random what the dominant people of the nineteenth century have written, and you will find at what conceptions man has actually arrived.

I have a book here before me; it is, in a certain sense, a book representing profoundly decisive views of the nineteenth century for it deals with the human soul. Every possible effort is made in this book to prove that this soul is something simply talked about by stupid people of earlier and present times. It was written in 1865, but these views were disseminated, and though some people say today that we have passed beyond that, we have not, but are still deep within it in the life of feeling and of general culture. The book deals with the human soul, but a special effort is made to demonstrate that the animal soul is the same as that of humans. In particular, you will find in it a neat definition of women and men. The author says that women represent in their peculiar characteristics a greater tendency to spirituality, whereas men represent more the tendency to materialism. In other words, according to this statement, spirituality is a weakness of women! The author then finds that certain crazy psychologists still speak about an ego that distinguishes man from animal. But he says in a delicate way that the cat, for example, shows that it also says ''I''; that it has the same kind of consciousness of the ego, so the author expresses it, as our vague and supersensible psychologists because the ego consciousness of the cat is not in the least different from that of the human being. Then comes a passage that is quoted from another book with which, however, the author is in full agreement. I shall read this passage, and I beg you to excuse the fact that the language is a bit off-color, but this is not my fault. It is the fault of the philosophy that has developed under such influences and that proposes to project living impulses into the future, asserting that it is the only philosophy today worthy of the human being. The passage reads:

The theologians and metaphysicians of our age pretend that man is the only religious animal. This is utterly false and the error is entirely in keeping with that made by some travelers who conclude, from the absence of organized cults, that religion is absent among certain savage peoples. Among a great proportion of the entire succession of animals, including even the molluscs, indications are to be found of fetishism and star worship. [So we find among the molluscs and other animals indications of fetishism and worship of the stars.] Those that most nearly approach the human being live in veritable polytheistic anthropolatry. Our domestic dog barks at the moon and howls in a particular way when it is at the seashore; it may also be seen on certain occasions making use of whatever lustral water is available and carrying out more or less obscure rites. Who would be able to prove that there have never been high priests among dogs? What could have degraded the poor animal to the point of causing him to lick the hand that strikes him if this was not done by religious and superstitious ideas? How is one to explain, except on the basis of a profound anthropolatry, the voluntary submission to man of so many animals stronger and more active than he? To be sure, it will be said that the animal frequently devours his god, but *primus in orbo deos fecit timor* (fear, first of all things on earth, created gods). . . . Besides, the sectarians of most of the religions also eat theirs!

The book in which this view is approved is entitled *Materialism and Spiritualism* and was written by Leblais[110] with a preface by Littré,[111] a man who produced a whole series of writings. In 1871 he was elected to the National Assembly and in the same year was made a member of the Academy. This same Littré, a man known throughout the entire world, wrote the preface to this book. It deals with the human soul and simply expresses in an emphatic way what in essence is pulsing through many souls today. It is only because people are so little inclined to observe life that they fail to see the important bearing it has upon the course of human evolution, to the sorrow and pain of anyone who sees into these things.

Thus, I wanted to present to you a by no means isolated example of the presence of materialistic views in the second half of the nineteenth century.

Now let us ask whether such views are without significance for external life. Do they not gradually penetrate into this external life? Do they not mold and form this external life? Just yesterday I was sent a book by a member, the young Swiss Albert Steffen[112], in which he could observe various currents of our time, because he is, in a certain sense, permeated by those impulses that are at play in spiritual science. Young Steffen describes a little of what can be experienced by a man who permits the influences of materialism on the molding of the social world to work upon him.

In his novel, which is called *The True Lover of Destiny (Der rechte Liebhaber des Schicksals)*, there is a character named Arthur who records a fragment of his life for a certain purpose. It is, to be sure, a section taken from a novel, but it describes much of what pulses today in life. So this Arthur describes a fragment from that part of his life when materialism takes hold of humanity and forms the social order. Arthur says:

> At twenty-one, I went to a metropolis for the first time —not the city in which I now live—in order to begin my studies.
>
> One the day of my arrival I took a look at the streets. It was raining. Everything was murky and dirty. The people all showed the same indifferent but hurried

162

pace, one just like another. I felt myself overcome immediately by an inner barrenness. I stopped in front of a billboard to see where I might spend the evening. I read one poster that called for a meeting in favor of prohibition. A man came with a pastepot and brush and pasted a beer bottle poster over it.

The very mark of our age—a poster in favor of anti-alcoholism with a beer bottle poster pasted over it!

Then suddenly I understood the significance of the mood that had taken possession of me since I arrived in this city: it was foolish to wish to improve human beings.

Disabled people stood to the right and left on the streets, yet no one had time to consider their misfortune. Women passed by and offered themselves and nobody showed pity or indignation. Suddenly it seemed to me almost astonishing that the shopkeepers did not come out of their shops to smash everything to pieces and shout, "What does it matter?" But then I perceived that the only reason that people did not despair was because they were already too commonplace, too cunning, too thievish. They were entirely too much at home in these alleys.

And did I then despair? I must confess that I greedily sucked up the mood of this alley. With a shuddering lust for death I took in the certainty that everything was on the way to destruction. The people who met me bore the unmistakable signs of degeneration. The houses reeked of corruption. Even the gray sky seemed to drop something heavy and inevitable from its clouds.

This feeling grew stronger in me. In this state of soul I sought out almost unconsciously darker and darker alleys. I went into courtyards full of refuse. I stared into windows and witnessed dreadful crimes. I read

163

the notices that swindlers and procuresses thrust into my hands. Finally, I climbed aboard one of the buses that roared with terrific power through the streets. I closed my eyes. The thundering noise rumbled through me like a hymn of death.

Suddenly the vehicle stopped. I stooped over and heard a few indifferent words. A child had run across the street, had been caught under a wheel and was carried away dead. We continued our way.

From this moment on something within me was paralyzed. I could now see the horrible thing that this city was, and it no longer horrified, angered, or disgusted me. It seemed to me quite natural.

More: I had to laugh at anybody who wanted to change it.

Could a person move otherwise in this fever of hunger, thirst, and passions?

My father came from a family of pastors. He studied natural science and absorbed its results with great enthusiasm. It made him clear in thought, thorough, broad-minded and, in the truest sense of the word, human. He applied all his powers to the investigation of the sensory world. The supersensible did not interest him. At least, I learned nothing of it from him.

In my childhood I adopted his view of the world without investigating whether its theories might be one-sided, just as an admiring child receives the truth from his father. But I did not yet possess his steadfastness of character that is acquired in the course of life, nor the religiousness he inherited from his ancestors, which he denied, but which was nonetheless in his nature. I did not have such a stock to live on. No pious practices were taught me in my youth that would have enriched

164

and deepened my soul and could have worked on further in me.

Now bear in mind how often I have said—I have brought this to your attention for years—that the first generation will still be able to live with materialism because it lives under the spiritual influence received from its forefathers, but that the succeeding generation would degenerate under materialism and would go to ruin. It is gratifying—if such a thing can be gratifying—that this truth passes over now even into literature. Steffen's narrator continues:

> Perhaps this is why the effect of scientific knowledge on me was different from what it was on my father. That inner inheritance prevented him from carrying over into life what he had attained as knowledge. In my case it was quite different; this single day had the effect of reversing, so to speak, the direction of my will.

> My father confessed to an intellectual satisfaction when he reflected that the human being is dissipated after death and no longer exists. The certainty of this, and it seemed certain to me, evoked in me a sort of ecstatic impulse to self-destruction and, as a result, heartlessness and lust for crime.

I recently pointed out to you that modern humanity is cruel even in its use of concepts. Now we read here:

> That evening I had become empty, void of feeling, and cruel, and I did not say *No* to these characteristics. In the succeeding time I lived entirely without scruple. And just because my action arose not from an impulse that I was unable to master, but from a certain logic and strength of will, the effect on me was twice as disastrous. I knew this. I was absolutely wicked.

He now relates how he fell into bad company, led another into bad company, and so forth. This you can read yourselves. But there is another brief passage to which I should like to call attention because it is symptomatic. A number of Arthur's acquaintances are together, all of them persons "worthy of honor," who intended the best within their group. But Arthur has to slip away on one occasion, and he then sits alone at an empty table. Steffan narrates the incident as follows:

> After a while a gentleman sat down opposite him whose face struck him because it bore an astonishing likeness to his own. It was pale, lean, smoothly shaven, but with somewhat more witch-like lines.
>
> A peddlar came, put his glasses on his nose, untied a bundle of picture postcards and, with a sleight-of-hand rapidity, put them first before Arthur, then before the stranger all the while looking into the face of the one under whose nose he held them as if he might see his chances there. Arthur turned away in disgust. The stranger went through them carefully and selected about ten, which he put together and tore to pieces. "These persons should not be given the opportunity to earn anything," he said to Arthur. "Of course, he will order a double supply of those I purchased. They were the most dreadful of all. But I saw so many decent working class couples here that I was afraid he would show these cards to them."
>
> "How can anyone look at such pictures?" asked Arthur.
>
> "Surrender yourself for a moment, without resistance, to the fumes in here, and you will see that figures take form in your soul whose movements are just as ugly as is depicted on the postcards. What are our places of entertainment today other than hells? You need only test your feelings after you have left them—smoke,

fumes, prostitutes. You do not take anything noble away with you."

"Why are you, then, in this dangerous place?" asked Arthur.

"Because I consider it necessary that someone should be here who is disgusted. The thought of the necessity for disgust in our time came to me a few days ago at an exhibit of Greek vases. The Greeks did not need to be disgusted in order to attain to beauty. They lived in it from the beginning. But we need this disgust if we wish to stand completely in life, in order to value the world correctly, in order to come to the spirit within us, in order to protect the God within us. It was different with the Greeks. When they surrendered themselves to life, they fulfilled also the laws of the spirit. They did not need to constantly defend and arm themselves. The work of man everywhere made the human being beautiful—the buildings, the art, the customs, the utensils, even to the smallest thing. But we become ugly through everything that surrounds us —streets, posters, movies, popular music—everything makes us barren, everything destroys us . . ."

Here is a question we must study: what lives at first in the thought world, and in the world of feeling, how does it flow into the social world? It is not good simply to sleep through life, not knowing what has been working at the bottom of it before it has come to its ultimate consequence. After all, the reason such a man, who has taken into himself something from spiritual science, describes this life well is because he has an eye for it.

IX

One of the criticisms that is made against our spiritual science by many theologians and others who believe they stand on a Christian foundation, but without understanding it correctly, is that spiritual science affirms truths regarding a large number of hierarchies that embrace beings standing above man in the spiritual world. We speak, as you know, of spiritual hierarchies embracing the angels, archangels, archai, exusiai, and so forth; we speak of these kingdoms of the higher supersensible worlds just as we speak of the animal, plant, mineral, and elemental kingdoms within the earthly world. It is quite clear to us, moreover, that human life falls into two sections. One of them takes its course between birth and death. During this life, or by reason of this life, man descends from the supersensible world to the kingdoms of the human being, and to those of the animal, plant, and mineral in his physical environment. When an individual passes through the portal of death, the other section of his life begins; he or she ascends to the higher kingdoms that tower upward from below just as the other kingdoms descend from above downward. The individual ascends into the kingdoms of the angels, archangels, archai, and so on. The person of the present day who believes, but without understanding, that his own foundation is that of Christianity is especially antagonistic to this view of the beings who have their place between man and the real Godhead, which is far above humanity and those beings who have their place in this supersensible space, i.e., the angels, archangels and so forth. Especially the people who believe themselves to be unusually advanced in their Christian conception will declare that this knowledge of the spiritual hierarchies and their beings represents a relapse into an ancient polytheism or, as it is said, into a kind of paganism. In their opinion it is precisely the mission of contemporary man to place nothing whatever between himself and the Godhead, but to live in the world directing his view to what is offered to the senses, and then to find his way directly to the Godhead without the mediation of angels, archangels, and so forth. Many people consider it especially sublime to stand thus, without mediation, face to face with their god.

You may hear this objection raised against spiritual science from many directions. It indicates that in those very circles there is absolutely no understanding of what the spiritual needs of our time really are, since it is not important if a man *imagines* he can find the way to his god, but rather whether he actually *can*. What is really important is not at all the question of whether the human being imagines he has a conception of his god, but whether he really does have such a conception. From our point of view, we must ask what the conception is that those individuals really hold when they say, "We do not wish any mediation by other spirits but will ascend directly from our souls to our god." What is the concept held by such men? Do they really have a conception of God when they speak of Him? When a man speaks of his god in a justifiable manner, does he conceive of what must be meant by the term *God*?

This is not the conception they hold, but rather something quite different. When we review all the concepts such individuals form of their god, what is really represented in such concepts? Nothing other than the being of an angel, and all those who say that they look up directly from their own souls to God are really looking only to an angel. If you examine all the descriptions given by such people, no matter how lofty they may seem, you will find that they describe nothing but an angel, and what they are saying is nothing more than to demand that one should conceive nothing higher under the term *God* than an angel. For example, what is called God in modern Protestantism, the God about whom there is so much talk among the protestants, is nothing other than one of the angels—nothing else whatever. The important fact is not whether a person imagines that he or she is finding the way to the highest God, but to what such a person really does find the way. Thus, in this manner, individuals find the way only to their own angel—I say to their *own* angel because that is important.

If we fix our attention first on the beings of the lowest hierarchies—archai (spirits of personality, as we have also named them), archangels and angels—then comes man, the animal kingdom, the plant kingdom and the mineral kingdom.

Archai	=	Spirits of Personality
Archangeloi	=	Archangels
Angeloi	=	Angels
		Man
		Animals
		Plants
		Minerals

When we direct our attention to these beings who are relatively the lowest, we need only bear in mind what has already been explained in order to know that the archai, the spirits of personality, are also time spirits. They are the controlling forces for the entire temporal epoch; they are what lives as spirit in a temporal epoch. We live today in a different spiritual relationship from that of the ancient Greeks or Romans because we are controlled by a different time spirit, who is, of course, a most sublime being. Then we have, in turn, those beings whom we call archangels whose mission is to establish harmony among men on earth; thus they are also, in a certain sense, the leaders and guides of peoples. The angels, standing just above man, guide and lead him through the portals of death so that he has his angel by his side from death to a new birth and is lead by him again into a new life. The mission of the angels is to guide individual humans through repeated earthly lives.

Now we have come all the way down to man. In his earthly existence today, man remembers only his life in the physical body. The memory of angels extends much further, and it is only through the far greater extension of their memory that they can guide and direct man's repeated earthly lives. But the modern theologian does not even conceive the angel correctly because he has eliminated the angels' characteristic of guiding the individual through repeated earthly lives. Let us grasp the fact that it is only the archangels who are beings who control human relationships over long stretches of time. Then, if we also conceive of angels as beings who really control the life of the individual, we shall readily acknowledge that it is a concealed egoism that makes people wish to ascend directly to their god. Although they do not admit it, the truth is that what they wish to do is to ascend only to their *own* god, to their own angel.

This has immense practical significance and is most important because it bears within it a certain germ in that men speak of one god, but he is nothing but a phantasm. The truth is that, in surrendering to this phantasm, each speaks of his own god; that is, of his angel. As a result, in the course of time each human being comes to worship his own god, that is to say, his own angel. We already see how strong is the impulse of humans each to worship his own god. During modern times, the union of human beings with those gods who are common to all has become quite restricted. The emphasis that each places upon his own god has become most conspicuous. Humanity has been fragmented into bits and pieces. All that survives is merely the *word* god, which has a common sound for the peoples using the same language, but each individual conceives something different in connection with this one word; that is, his own angel. He does not even ascend to the archangel who guides society.

At the bottom of this lies a certain concealed egoism but people will not admit it. When we consider this, however, we see it is an important statement because a man really lives in an untruth when he denies that he looks up to *his angel* while declaring that he looks up to the *one and only god*. He lives in a nebulous conception; that is, an inner illusion, an inner maya, and this has important consequences. When we surrender ourselves to this inner illusion and to fantastic conceptions, we do not all change the spiritual realities that come about by virtue of our correct or incorrect conception. As a human being really looks up to his angel but does not admit this, believing on the contrary that he is looking up to God, while really not looking up even to an archangel, he deadens his soul by means of this untruthful conception. This stupefaction of the soul is everywhere present nowadays but, when the soul is stupefied, the consequences for human evolution are disastrous. This is so because the deadening of the soul brings about a suppression of the ego, a beclouding of the ego, and then other forces that ought not to work in the soul do actually slip in. That is to say, in place of the angel, whom the person at first wanted to revere but whom he wrongly names "God," the *luciferic angel* slips in and it gradually comes about that the individual reveres not the angel, but the luciferic angel. Then, however, the steep incline is near that leads man downward because he is close to the utter denial of God; that is, the denial of his own angel, which is always connected with the denial of the true ego. I have shown you an example of this in the book by Leblais, *Materialism and*

Spiritualism, where it is asserted that the cat has an ego just as a human being does, and where the author speaks of the "high priest of the dogs"!

Thus, we must understand that, from many points of view, the answer to the question: Who is to blame for the materialism of our time? must be: The religions are to blame, the religious sects. They darken the consciousness of man and put in the place of God an angel who is then replaced by a corresponding luciferic angel. The latter will soon lead the human being into materialism. This is the mysterious connection among proud egoistic religious sects who are unwilling to listen to anything that stands above the angelic level, but assert with boundless pride that they are speaking of God, whereas they are speaking only of an angel, and incompletely at that. In the final analysis, this incredible arrogance, which is often called humility, was bound to bring on materialism. When we bear this in mind, we see a highly significant connection; that is, through the false interpretation of one's angel as God, the inclination to materialism arises in the human soul. There is an unconscious egoism lying at the bottom of this that is expressed through the fact that the human being disdains to ascend to a knowledge of the spiritual world and hopes to find a direct connection with his god only out of himself. When you pay close attention to what I have here suggested, you will gain an insight into much that plays a part in the present. There is only one single way of avoiding misinterpretation of God and that is to acknowledge the spiritual hierarchies. We then know that the present religious denominations do not rise any higher than to the hierarchy of the angels.

As we consider this, we are standing more or less within the realm of what a person develops in conscious life, but much that lives in the human being is also unconscious, or not clearly conscious. Now we might say that the connection between an individual and his or her angel is a real one,

173

but then so is one's connection with the hierarchy of the archangels and that of the archai. The misinterpretation of the angel, which is performed more or less consciously, leads also more or less consciously to a materialistic conception of the world, not in the case of the individual human being but gradually over a period of time. When we are talking about an individual's relation to his angel, we are still dealing in some way with conscious processes of the human soul. But in the relationship of the human being to the hierarchy of the archangels, we already stand in the midst of something of which man knows little; something of which he speaks a great deal at times but regarding which he knows almost nothing. Nowadays, to be sure, we have confessions directed not to the hierarchy of the archangels but frequently to *one* archangel—not a clearly expressed confession but the inclination of the feeling nature to one or another of the archangels. At least in one field this bore obvious fruit during the nineteenth century: in the rise of the idea of nationality. This idea is grounded in an unconscious desire to overlook the cooperation among the archangels and instead, be inclined to always embrace a single archangel. Something egoistic lies at the basis of this as is the case with man's inclination to a single angel, but here the egoism is of a social nature.

Now, we might well desire to describe what arises in connection with this social-egoistic inclination to an archangel, just as materialism arises consciously in connection with the misinterpretation of the angel. But here we walk on slippery ice and it is not possible to speak of it in our day.

Still more obscure are the relationships of the human being to the archai, the time spirits. These relationships are subliminal in nature. Human beings do stand at least in a sort of relationship to angels. Even though they do not admit it, yet, when they say, "I believe in God," they admit this in the false way I have indicated. But if they at least

174

desire to establish a relationship to the angels, their attempted relationship to the archangels in their feelings and
emotions is not in tune with the spirit of our times. When
they claim they have a certain connection by reason of their
blood or something of the kind, this connection at the present time is false. This leads to false paths that I will not, cannot, describe today, but they are similar to the ones they en-
counter when they deal with the spirits of a time. People
will embrace them in the forms in which the spirit of their
own time presents itself to them. Just bear in mind how we
endeavor by means of spiritual science to oppose this egoistic representation when we describe the consecutive periods
of time with their special characteristics, letting them work
upon us. By this, our hearts and souls may be broadened to
extend over the entire evolution of the earth, indeed, over
the entire cosmic evolution, attaining thereby, at least in our
thoughts, a relation to the various time spirits. But people
today will not have this. Much that has only been suggested
would have to be described if we should wish to picture
those false ways upon which men enter because of this egoism in reference to the spirit of the time. I have been able to
give you from a work of fiction[113] a dark picture, described
in a remarkable fashion, of our immediate present. Such
false paths as are there described are connected with this
false relationship to the spirit of the time. But as we encoun-
ter these false paths in relation to the time spirit, we enter
into a most important realm. When a human being who
substitutes his angel for God passes from his angel to a luciferic angel, it is a confusion in belief, in acknowledgment of
a world conception, which is, in a sense, individual. Next
there may be a confusion of entire peoples; nevertheless, it
remains an aberration among human beings in a certain
way, and the consequences can always be blamed on human
aberrations. But when we advance to the spirit of the time
and fall into error in relation to it, we then collide with the

cosmos in our errors. There is a mysterious relationship between errors related to the time spirit and the beginnings of what man brings down upon himself cosmically. A person disinclined to look up to anything above the angel sees nothing of this connection. What I am now saying let each of you receive as best you can. It is asserted from spiritual science and profound investigations, but I would have to speak for months if I wanted to place these investigations before you in detail.

The errors the human being perpetrates in relation to the spirit of the time clash with cosmic events and these cosmic events strike back. The result of their being brought into human life—at first, their beginnings—is decadence that extends even to the physical body, bringing diseases and mortality and all that is connected with them. Perhaps in a not too distant future humanity will be convinced that much that man performs on the physical plane, when it is of such a nature as to transgress even all the way to the time spirit, evokes destructive forces in earthly evolution whose influences extend even to illness and death. If you ask yourselves on the basis of insights you have acquired, whether much of what has been happening recently may not constitute a violation of the time spirit, you will be able to answer that these profound connections extending to illness and death introduce a compensation for all sorts of sins perpetrated against the time spirit.

We know perfectly well that the clever men of the present will, of course, only laugh when such things are asserted. They know, on the basis of their scientific view of the world, that it is mere nonsense, as they say, to suppose that what a human being does, what men do in their relationships, could cause events to occur in the elemental sphere. But the time is not far distant when men will believe this simply because they will be able to see it.

What is lacking in our age for a real view of the world,

capable of supporting human life, is seriousness. It is for this reason that one of the first demands made upon those who enter spiritual science is to develop this seriousness in their view of the world and really to penetrate the course of human evolution a little. We have frequently emphasized the fact that the evolution of the world really acquires meaning only through the Mystery of Golgotha, and we have already introduced many considerations that revealed the Mystery of Golgotha in its deeply significant light. But our characterization must become ever more thorough if we wish to comprehend the complete significance of this event. The question may be asked how the human soul then really reaches Christ. It may be said that, since Christ is, of course, a Being higher than all the archai, the way to Christ must be found. The paths that are used today by the ordinary religious confessions do not lead to the Christ but at most to an angel, as we have seen. People may conduct themselves as they do today in the names of various angels or even archangels, if the luciferic beings have taken the place of the progressive beings. But one cannot so conduct oneself in the name of the Christ since it is an absolute impossibility for two human beings who are hostile to one another to confess the Christ. I think this is not difficult to see because it is self-evident. This is possible when a person utters the name, *Christ, Christ*, or *Lord, Lord*—as Christ indicated—and means only his or her own angel, but it is impossible when a person is really speaking of Christ. So the question may arise as to how, indeed, the soul comes to a path leading to the Christ. We may approach the solution to this problem in various ways and shall here enter upon a road we have come to in a natural way from many considerations.

People today know extremely little of the past. Least of all do they know why certain things have been handed down. At best, they know they have been handed down but they scarcely know why. Tradition reports, for example—this may be read in all sorts of esoteric books even including those on Freemasonry—that there were mysteries in ancient times. They were a secret institution in which the mysteries, as even the name suggests, contained secrets that were really so also in the external sense. That is, one who had found access to the mysteries was informed about certain things that he was obligated not to communicate except to those who, in turn, were associated with him in these mysteries; it was a stringent rule that these msytery communications should not be betrayed. It was one of the most punishable misdeeds should one utter a mystery secret within hearing distance of the uninitiated, but it was just as punishable an offense were one to listen who was not qualified to hear it. As long as the mysteries existed in the ancient sense, this rule was observed in the strictest way. Why was this? Why did it happen in this way?

You see, there is a good deal of talk today about the mysteries, especially on the part of people who utter all sorts of pretty words and who wish to whine a little through what they say. Especially where there is much talk about these things without the necessary will to understand much, as is frequently the case among the Masons, a great deal of nonsense is practiced; people talk superficially about these things without knowing too much. They do not notice whether these things are discussed on the basis of facts or whether the talk is nothing but words. We may have the most astonishing experiences in connection with these things, which I do not wish in the least to criticize or rebuke, but the matter is too serious to be left without some mention of it. For instance, the following may occur. Someone or other is a member of one of the societies that are called by all kinds of fraternal names and claim to be protectors of the mysteries. Such a person—and I am telling you facts —comes to you and asks for information about something seemingly of interest to him—at least, in words—but which he can little understand. Later, it is reported that he has been making speeches here and there about these things and that what he has said has been more or less worthless. To these very miseducated persons who have been spoiled by certain occult brotherhoods, it is most futile of all to speak because they do not enter into what is really important. Only in this way could it recently happen, for example, that a book was published by a well-known lecturer and writer, a free thinker regarding the secrets of Freemasonry, that naturally contains nothing whatever but the shallowest stuff. This nonsense is taken seriously even by those who belong to so-called occult brotherhoods.

Now we will bring to mind a real characteristic in connection with the practices of the mysteries that has grown from the evolution of humanity. I have frequently stressed the fact that humanity has changed in the course of earthly evolution and that an important incision occurred in this evolution at the time when Christ passed through the Mystery of Golgotha. If we wish to consider a vitally important characteristic of this evolution along with others we have already mentioned, we must say that, when we go back beyond the Greco-Latin period and especially if we should pass beyond the fourth century before Christ all the way into the fifth, sixth and seventh centuries—we might even remain within the Greco-Latin but we should find more if we entered into the Egypto-Chaldean or even passed all the way to the Persian—we find everywhere that what was uttered by men had an entirely different significance for the rest of mankind from what it possessed, for example, even in the seventh and eighth centuries after the Mystery of Golgotha. The words that one person spoke to another had an entirely different meaning during the time when the ancient atavistic characteristics of the soul, leading all the way even to atavistic clairvoyance, were still present from what it had

179

later, even today. At that time the word possessed, by reason of its inner power, a sort of suggestive quality; there dwelt in it much inherited divine-spiritual power. When the human being spoke, his angel also spoke in a certain way from the higher hierarchies.

From this fact you can imagine that oral communications in those ancient times were something wholly unlike those of our day. Even if we knew all these mysteries, it would be impossible for us to express ourselves now in words as it was possible in ancient times because in speaking with words we must speak with what they have become through language. Indeed, in words we have conventional signs. We can no longer go to the human being and, with the same power with which one could still speak of Christ in the third, fourth, or fifth centuries, cause a gentle tremor that was a healing force to pass through his soul by means of the words, "Thine angel holds thee dear." That can no longer be done today; words have lost their ancient suggestive quality, their power. When human beings spoke to one another in ancient times, the power of human fellowship streamed from soul to soul. Just as we breathe the same air when we sit together in a hall, so did a spiritual power of what they were in common live in what human beings said to one another. As evolution has advanced, this has been lost. The word has been rendered ever less divine.

If you let your spiritual eye dwell upon this truth, you will be able to say that there might have been certain combinations of words, certain word formulas, that had a greater effect than others that were in general oral use. Such word formulas, possessing a power far surpassing that of other words, were communicated in the mysteries. Because these formulas gave the person who knew them a lofty power over other humans, you can now understand that they could not be disclosed or misused. It is an absolute fact that when an ancient Hebrew temple priest uttered in the right way what was ordinarily called the Word, but which was a certain combination of sounds, it then came about that, since in ancient times the force lay in this combination of sounds, a different world surrounded the human beings to whom he spoke; that is, in a spiritual sense, but this spirituality was real.

You can understand, therefore, that it was not only a criminal act to speak the mystery formulas to one to whom they should not be spoken since a certain domination was thus exercised over him that was unjustifiable, but it was also frowned upon to listen because a person thus exposed himself to the danger of being given over completely into the power of the other person. These things are not so abstract as certain persons wish to represent them; they are concrete and real. It is the times that have changed and it is necessary to pay attention to this. Since the Mystery of Golgotha, words no longer possess this significance; otherwise, as you can easily see, real freedom could not have arisen among human beings; in a way, their souls would have remained nothing but the product of speech. Words had to lose this inner force. But another power then entered into earthly evolution that could gradually return to men what originally came from words if only they should find the right relationship to it. The people of ancient times learned to think from their words, and there were no other thoughts in ancient times than those that came from words. But the power of thoughts could come from words only if they were of the character I have described. In later times this power was no longer present. But then He came, that Being who could again restore this force to thoughts if they were filled with Him, that Being who could say, "I am the Word." This is the Christ. But men must first find the way to make Christ live in their souls. The Christ is there. We know that since the time of the Mystery of Golgotha He is a real power. Now, while we are speaking about karma, we also want to show how He has a relationship to it. An angel enters into relationship with the single man alone, but the Christ can have a far higher significance than even an archangel since He not only united men here on earth in accordance with the time spirit but also unites the living with the dead; in other words, He unites those souls who are here organized in their bodies and also those who have already passed through the portal of death. We must learn, however, to understand a little better how the Christ can be found in the spirit of our times; that is, how a way to Him can be found, since we began with the question, "How can the human being find a way to the Christ today?"

Above all other things, it is necessary that man should once more rise above the egoistic habit of living only in his own soul. A word of truth in the Gospels—and how many words that we read in the Gospels are not taken according to their true meaning because they do not please us—a word of truth in the Gospels is, "Where two or three are gathered in My name, there am I in the midst of them."[114] The spirit of vain mysticism that says, "The Christ shall be born in my soul," is not the spirit of Christianity; that spirit declares, "Where two or three are gathered in My name, there am I in the midst of them." However, in order to explain the entire spirit of this saying in connection with repeated earthly lives, as we wish to do in these reflections, and also in connection with the vocational life of a human being today, I must discuss something especially characteristic of our age. We must learn to rise above the egoistic limitation within our human nature. In a sense applicable to our time, we must rise above this by learning once again to know and think of the cosmos with which the human being is related and from which he is born by learning to think of it in relation to man.

Do you believe that today's science is capable of thinking of the cosmos in relation to man? Recall the assertion of Hermann Grimm that I have quoted even in public lectures, "Natural scientists conceive of a sort of mechanism in which the human being cannot possibly exist."[115] It is entirely impossible today for the scientific view of the world for one to think of man in relation to the cosmos. This cannot be done unless we first learn to view things concretely. Someone constructs a machine today and believes that nothing further has really happened than the actual construction or what will be brought about by means of it. But to give oneself up to such a belief means to establish what may be called negative superstition, and it is most widespread. Superstition is the belief in spirits when none exist, but a person may also express a disbelief in spirits when they are present, and this is negative superstition. Humanity abandons itself completely to this negative superstition without really knowing it because it is not yet accustomed to think of the things that enter human evolution as being cosmically interrelated and under a moral point of view. They are considered only as a mechanism.

Let us select a single example but one that is characteristic of our age and similar to much else that dominates our external life; that is, the steam engine. What a role is played today by the steam engine! Just think for a moment of how many things would not exist if there were no steam engine. I will not say that everything men have must be produced by it, but much is brought about by this machine that is in accord with the true spirit of the age.

The steam engine was really not produced until the eighteenth century. What existed before that time constituted nothing more than impractical experiments. In other words, we may say that the enormously significant steam engine that is used universally today was first made applicable in 1719 by Newcomen[116] and then later, in 1762, by Watt.[117]

We can speak of these two as the originators of it, at least in the sense in which today we speak of it and everything connected with it.

Now, what makes it possible for us to have steam engines, which are by no means old? What is the basis of this possibility? You see, the year 1769—I shall now make an assertion that will seem extremely curious to everyone who thinks scientifically—when Watt first made the steam engine useful, was a year by no means far removed from Goethe's conception of the *Faust*. Although they lie far apart, perhaps we might discover in our reflections curious interrelationships between this steam engine and the conception of Goethe's *Faust*. But we must first survey in thought much that is connected with the introduction of the steam engine into human evolution. On what principle does the steam engine actually rest? It really rests on the possibility of creating space void of air, or occupied by little of it. The entire possibility of making steam engines rests on the creation and use of a vacuum. In ancient times men spoke of the *horror vacui*, the horror of a vacuum. Something objective was indicated thereby. It meant that space wants always to be filled with something; that something empty could really not be produced; that nature had a certain horror of a vacuum. First, the belief in the horror of a vacuum had to disappear. Secondly, the possibility had to be established that space containing little air or being almost void of air, could be created. Only then was it possible to consider the use of steam engines. The air had to be eliminated from certain spaces. It is not possible through a mechanical consideration to attain to a new cosmic, moral conception in contrast with the ancient cosmic and moral conception of the *horror vacui*. But what really happens when we create a space containing little or no air with the purpose of placing what is thus brought about in the service of human evolution?

The ancient Biblical narrative declares that Jahve

breathed the living breath, the air, into man, and he became thereby a living soul. Air had to be introduced into man in order for him to become what he ought as an earthly human being. For many hundreds and even thousands of years, man made use of only that rarefaction and condensation of air that occurred automatically in a cosmic connection. Then came the modern age when man undertook to rarefy the air, to put away what Jahve had put in, to work in opposition to the manner in which Jahve can work in placing humans on the earth. What really happens when man makes use of space containing little air, that is, drives air out of space? Here opposition occurs against Jahve. You may now easily think that, whereas Jahve streams into man through air, man drives Jahve out when he creates a space containing rarefied air. When the steam engine is created in this way, Ahriman gains the possibility of establishing himself as a demon even in the very physical entity. In constructing steam engines, the condition is created for the incarnation of demons. If anyone is unwilling to believe in them, he need not do so; that is negative superstition. Positive superstition consists in seeing spirits where there are none; negative superstition consists in denying spirits where they are. In steam engines ahrimanic demons are actually brought even into a physical object. That is, while the cosmos has descended with its spiritual element through what has been poured into human evolution, the spirit of the cosmos is driven out through what is created in the form of demons. That is to say, this new, important and wonderful advance has brought about not only a demonology, but also a demon magic that frequently imbues modern technology.

Many things, and here again I make a somewhat paradoxical statement, become manifest when we learn rightly to read what is often considered least significant. After all, this (here the letter *i* was first written on the blackboard without a dot, and later a dot was placed over it) is the prin-

185

cipal part even of the material substance of this letter, but only the dot makes it the letter *i*. Consider how much less this dot contains than the other part even though it is the dot that makes the letter. The person who clings only to the material element in the evolution of humanity will also frequently see even in the material only what contains a hundred times as much as the dot and will fail entirely to see the dot. But one who observes more closely, who does not merely stare at the phenomena but reads them, will often learn to read things in the right way when a delicate suggestion is made. It is astonishing that in a biography of James Watt you will find mention of the following fact; I shall refer to it in a way that will seem utterly insane to every modern and intelligent person. But of course, you yourselves must first understand the interpretation of this fact. Watt could not at first accomplish what he intended through his invention, his steam engine. You see, its development stretched from 1712 to 1769. When once a man has invented something, others, of course, imitate it again and again. Thus much was constructed between these two dates. When Watt had finally made his machine really workable by means of other improvements, he had used a contrivance in it for which someone else held a patent; because of this, he could not proceed until he had thought out something different to replace it. He then discovered what he needed in a strange way. He was living, of course, in an age in which the Copernican view of the world had long been held, which I have characterized as something suitable for the spirit of our age alone. It actually occurred to him to construct his mobile apparatus in such a way that he could call it the "movement of the sun and the planets." He spoke of it thus because he was really guided by what is conceived in the Copernican system as the revolution of the planets around the sun. He had actually brought down and concealed within the steam engine what had been learned in the modern age as the movement of the heavenly bodies.

Now, bear in mind what I recently explained as something that will happen but which is at present only in its beginnings; that is, that delicate vibrations will accumulate and tremendous effects will thus be produced. Thank God, it has not yet been achieved! But the beginning lies in the fact that the movement of the sun and the planets is copied. Since the movements of the sun and the planets possess a profound significance for our earth when they radiate inward, do you believe that they possess no significance when we copy them here in miniature and cause them to radiate outward again into cosmic space? What then happens has profound significance for the cosmos. Here you see directly how even those vibrations I spoke of are now added to the demon through which he can unfold his activity outward into cosmic space.

Of course, no one should suppose that what I have just said indicates that steam engines should be done away with. In that case one would have also to do away with a good deal more because they are by no means the most demoniacal. Whenever electricity is used—and much else besides—there is far more of demon magic because this operates with entirely different forces having an entirely different significance for the cosmos. Obviously, anyone who understands spiritual science will realize quite clearly that these things should not be done away with, that we cannot be reactionary or conservative in the sense that we must be opprsed to progress. Indeed, the demon magic signifies progress, and the earth will continue to make more and more progress. Developments in the world soon will make it possible to produce immense effects ranging outward into the universe. Doing away with these things or condemning them is not what we are after because they are obviously justified. But what must be borne in mind is that since they must appear on the one side in the course of human progress, counter forces must be created on the other to reestablish a balance. Counter forces must be created. They must bring about a balance that can be created only if humanity again comes to understand the Christ principle, if humanity finds the way to Christ. For a time humanity has been led away from the Christ. Even those who call themselves the official representatives of the Christ seek an angel instead of Him. But the way the soul must take to the Christ must be found. Just as we work all the way to the physical stars and into the cosmos by means of the demons of the machines, so must we find the way spiritually into the worlds in which human beings live between death and a new birth where the beings of the higher hierarchies are to be found. What I am now alluding to is connected with what I have already explained. Human beings enter more and more into a vocational karma on the one side, as I have explained, and from the other this vocational karma must be counteracted by an understanding of the spiritual world, which in turn can prepare them to find a way to Christ.

We will speak further of these things tomorrow.

X

When we seek the answer to the question to which we referred in the last lecture as to how human beings may establish a relationship with the Christ today, the objection is made by many that a number of human beings already have a relationship with Him. I have spoken frequently about this objection, and we know that it is invalid. On more careful consideration, it turns out to be a thoroughly egoistic objection that can be made only by a person who has the following view: "I have a faith that makes me happy; anything else is no concern of mine." But in general, humanity's relation to the Christ-Being is not satisfactory; that is easily recognizable from the events of our times and little needs to be added. The necessary answer to this objection can be given by everyone by saying that a basic element in the confession of Christ must be the truth that He died and rose for all men—for all men alike—and that, when man turns against man for the sake of external possessions, it can never be done in His name. It is possible for a person to turn away from this general human destiny to apply himself solely in egoistic fashion to his own creed. Certainly, but then no attenion is paid to the fact that the occurrence of the Mystery of Golgotha is something that primarily concerns human society. We will now have to mention something that may draw our attention to what is essential in the path that leads to Christ, since it is obvious that each soul must find the way to Him for himself with those means that are suitable for the present time.

When we seek to understand in a more profound sense

what the Christ Being signifies for the earth, we must first acquaint ourselves with the truth of an essential element in the Mystery of Golgotha; that is, it actually occurred only *once* at a definite point in space and time. When we fix this in our minds, we shall discover a contradiction of a view that is generally held, even by us; we should not simply seek to remove it by argumentation since it is justifiable and must first be recognized if we desire to remove it for our own souls. You see, provided the Mystery of Golgotha is an inner and genuine truth, it cannot represent anything but the meaning of the evolution of the earth. But, as we know, everything that occurs in time and space belongs to the realm of maya, the great illusion; that is, it does not belong to the real and eternal, the essential nature of things. Thus we face the highly significant contradiction that the Mystery of Golgotha belongs to maya, the great illusion, and we must place this contradiction before our souls in its full validity.

Now, since this Mystery of Golgotha occurred during the time of the earthly evolution of humanity, let us first consider this evolution. We know, of course, that what we have to deal with is that the human being has come over from earlier worlds and that at a definite point of time, as we have set forth in my book, *An Outline of Occult Science*, he was subjected to what may be called a luciferic temptation, a seduction. We have often considered this luciferic seduction in the sense in which spiritual scientific investigation shows it, and we know it was expressed in a magnificent image at the beginning of the Old Testament. In the so-called "Fall of Man," the image of Lucifer as a serpent in Paradise is one of the mightiest representations of religious documents.

When we survey the time through which humanity passed from the luciferic temptation to the Mystery of Golgotha, we find it to be a time in which human beings gradually descended from a primeval, atavistic clairvoyant, revelation

190

that was brought over from earlier planetary stages in which the spiritual worlds had a real existence before their souls. During the centuries preceding the Mystery of Golgotha, therefore, they were no longer able to look up to the spiritual world as they had done before, but they now possessed only echoes of the ancient knowledge of the spiritual world.

Taking now a relatively short period of earthly time since we cannot go all the way back to the luciferic temptation, let us review the successive descending stages of human evolution down to the Mystery of Golgotha. If we go back far enough, we discover that what men possessed at an earlier time as an atavistic wisdom, as a real perception of the spiritual world, now echoed in the world conceptions of the religions as reverence for a more or less significant, but highly regarded, ancestor. That is to say, in various regions of the earth we find religious cults that we may call ancestral cults. Such cults in which men look up with reverence to an ancestor still survive among those who have remained at a more or less early stage of evolution. What is the reason for this adoration? What is the reality behind this looking up to an ancestor in ancient times? In those most ancient times to which history can still look back, in that hoary antiquity, we have a certain epoch in which ancestral cults are customary (cf. chart on p. 194).

Such ancestral cults were not based on fact, as is supposed by superficial contemporary science, that those belonging to them imagined they had to look up to a certain ancestor, but the nature of the most ancient ancestral cults was such that men had a direct vision of their ancestors at a certain time in their lives. At these times, in a state of consciousness between waking and sleeping such as was universal in the earlier stages of human evolution, a person who looked up to an ancestral god really attained a condition of union with what he reverenced as his ancestor. The ancestor appeared to him not merely in a dream, but in a dream-like

191

image that signified something real to him, and those individuals to whom the same ancestor appeared belonged together in a single ancestral cult. What these individuals
beheld in spirit was, to be sure, a human form elevated to a
lofty level, but something entirely different was concealed
behind it. If we wish to know what was really concealed
behind this spirit form, we must realize that the ancestor
had once died and had left the earth as a highly regarded
personality who had wrought much good for a human community. He had passed through the portal of death and
when these individuals looked up to him, he was on the way
between death and a new birth. As these human beings
looked up to him, what was it they saw of him?

We know, of course, that when a human being passes
through the portal of death, he remains for a short time in
his etheric body before it is cast off. But the casting off of
this body signifies that it passes over into the spiritual
worlds, into the etheric world. The human being continues
to develop in his ego and his astral body; the etheric body
passes over into the etheric world. Since this man had performed something lasting on earth, the memory of his
etheric body continued for a long time. It is this etheric
body of the ancestor that was beheld in the ancient atavistic,
dream-like clairvoyance and people revered what was
revealed to them through it. But during the period between
death and a new birth, this etheric body comes into contact
with the spirits of the higher hierarchies; most particularly
with those belonging to the hierarchy of the archai, the spirits of time. Since this particular ancestor was a significant
personality for human evolution, he thus established a
union with the time spirit who was bringing human evolution one step forward.

What made itself known through this ghost, as we may
call it, of the ancestor was, in reality, one of the time spirits;
so worship within the most ancient religions was really

directed to the time spirit. Wherever we go back into those times that we may look upon as the hoary antiquity of history, we find that human beings worshipped the etheric bodies of their forefathers to cause the time spirits to reveal themselves. That is to say, as we go back to the ancestral cults, what we find is the worship of the time spirits, the archai.

Men then descended further and began to worship those gods who are known to us from the various mythologies, and whom we call archangels; even Zeus in Greek mythology possessed archangelic manifestations. In the most ancient times people looked up to the time spirits; later, they looked up to those spirits who are not time spirits but are of equal value with the spirits who control the guidance of different peoples, the archangels. Thus we may say that polytheism, when human beings worshipped archangels, follows after ancestral worship.

Then human beings descend still further to the period in which the ego is gradually to be born in the individual. We now find that the most advanced nations pass over to monotheism at a relatively early period—the Egyptians, for example, even in the second millennium before Christ, the people of the Near East later. That is, they begin to worship angels, every person his or her own angel, rather than an archangel. They descend from the higher polytheism to the lower monotheism. After what has previously been presented to you, you will not consider what I am about to say as something strange. You will see that people must cure themselves of the pride that permeates the entire field of religious studies, which deems itself justified to consider monotheism as a religion superior to polytheism. By no means is it so, but the relationship of the two is just as has been described.

Why, then, could the ancient peoples still worship archai, archangels, and angels? They could do so because

they still preserved a remnant or echo of the atavistic clairvoyant capacity. For this reason they were able to lift
themselves up to what is superhuman; they could, in a certain sense, rise above the human and elevate themselves to
the superhuman. In the ancient mysteries, this process of
elevating oneself to the superhuman was especially cultivated. Human beings were developed so they could unfold
within themselves what extended beyond the human,
whereby the human soul lifted itself into the realm of spirituality. But then came the time when the human ego, as it
lives here between birth and death, was born for human beings. This was the period coinciding with the occurrence of
the Mystery of Golgotha. If the Mystery of Golgotha had
not occurred, people would have degenerated; they would
have descended from worshipping angels to worshipping
the next subordinate hierarchy, man himself. When we
recall how the Roman Caesars had themselves worshipped
as gods, how they really were "gods" to the people, we shall
know that at the time of the Mystery of Golgotha human beings had degenerated so far that they now no longer prayed
to archai, archangels, or angels, but to man. In order to save
men from praying to earthly human beings, it was necessary
for the Divine Man to appear.

Archai Spirits of Time	Archangels	Angels	Man
Ancestor Worship	Polytheism	Monotheism	Divine Man

The entrance of the Divine Man into history signified an
important new way to relate oneself to religious life. Where
had the worship of angels, archangels, archai, and even that
of man in the form of the Roman Caesars, been found? In
man himself; no one worshipped the Caesars through the
Caesars, but through the worshipper himself, obviously;

194

this had arisen from man; it came from the human soul. It was necessary that the Christ should appear as historic fact in the evolution of humanity; it was necessary that He should be seen, like the phenomena of nature, from without. He had to come into touch with human beings in an entirely different way from that of the gods of the ancient religions—in an entirely different way. "Where two or three are gathered in My name, there am I in the midst of them." This is an important principle in Christianity because it signifies that, whereas it is possible through mere individual mysticism to find angels, archangels, even archai, it is not possible by this individual mysticism to find the Christ. Those who wish to practice individual mysticism, as this is often described even among theosophists, generally reach only the individual angel. They simply internalize this angel more, even making him often somewhat more egoistic than other persons make their gods. The Christ is found in different ways, not through the mere development of one's inner being, but when we are most of all aware that the Christ belongs to the community of human beings, to the whole of human community.

We now come to a most important differentiation, which can be taken into the human mind, we must admit, only with great difficulty. It is imperative, however, that we force ourselves to its level. When we face another human being in life, it is in maya that we, as human beings, face each other. Just as we have before us only the maya of natural phenomena, so are we likewise confronted only with the maya of the other human being. It is within maya that this human being stands before our external senses and all that is connected with the external world of the senses; then he stands before us as belonging to his family, his nation, his time. If we should survey him completely, we should see behind him the angel, the archangel, the archai, but they all express themselves in what the person is. It is because the

195

archangel and the archai stand behind the observer and the human being observed, the latter is in a sense a member of certain human groups. In other words, the observed person in this way stands within heredity and hereditary relationships. Only our shortness of vision—understandable because we are human—prevents us from consciously judging a human being before us according to these essential connections; unconsciously we always do this. Unconsciously we face one another within this differentiation, which must inevitably be brought into humanity by these three hierarchies. But the Christ demands something more, something different. He demands in reality that when you face someone, you shall feel that what such a human being appears to you to be in the external world is not the entire and complete human being. When you face a human being, you should perceive his or her real being as coming not only from archai, archangels and angels, but from higher spirits no longer belonging to the earthly or even planetary evolution because this begins with the archai, the higher heavenly spirits, as you know from *An Outline of Occult Science.* You must see that with the human being something enters into maya that is supramundane.

To understand fully what I have just expressed, you must not allow it to remain a mere concept but carry it over completely into your feelings. It is necessary to understand clearly that in every human being something supramundane in his nature comes to meet us, something not to be understood by earthly human means. Then everyone will experience that sensitive reverence in the presence of all that is human. Before the Mystery of Golgotha, man had gradually lost this superhuman element and had descended all the way to being human. The superhuman element had been lost because—listen carefully—when a human being such as a Roman Caesar comes to be worshiped as a god, he loses his humanity and sinks to the level of the subhuman. He ceases to be a human being if he permits himself to be worshipped as something superhuman in social life. Man was threatened, therefore, with the loss of his humanity and it was restored to him through the appearance of Christ on earth. Read the cycle of lectures, *From Jesus to Christ*,[118] in which I spoke on this question, telling you that something is really imparted to every individual human being through the fact that Christ was on earth.

Thus, the coming of the Christ has brought it about that we recognize in every earthly human being, even if he is a sinner or a publican, the Christ who is behind him. The Christ sat down with sinners so that we shall recognize in every earthly human being the truth of the statement, "What thou dost to the least of My brethren, thou has done unto Me."[119] As I have said, this concept must be transferred entirely into our feeling nature; only then shall we attain to its full truth. Then one also sees all concepts and ideas that separate men from one another fall away, and something belonging to all men in common spreads as an aura over the entire earth when we vow that we shall carry our search, not merely to the archai, but upward to what stands above them whenever we are in the presence of a human being.

If we look back again to the ancient mysteries, we find that in them the human being endeavored to transcend his own being in order to have his soul coalesce with the spiritual world. But through the occurrence of the luciferic temptation this is only partially possible. In this ascent the possibility is lost to ascend still further. It is not possible to bear anything more up into the higher world. Why is this so? The answer to this question will come to us if we fix our attention on the profounder meaning of the luciferic temptation. What does Lucifer truly purpose for humanity? We have often emphasized this. Humanity lives in maya, something that is not the real world but only a mirror of it. What, then, is Lucifer's intention? In this mirror the human being can lift himself up a few stages as far as to the archai, but he must then be taken over by Lucifer if he desires to rise still higher into the spiritual. In a certain sense, he must then take Lucifer as his guide; Lucifer, who constitutes the light that guides him further. If the luciferic evolution had continued, if Christ had not entered into human evolution, the following would have come about after the time in which the Mystery of Golgotha ought to have taken place: human beings within the mysteries would have developed to such an extent that the archai would have been openly visible to them. Then they would have entered into the luciferic world. In that case, however, all that the higher gods such as the exusiai implanted into earthly evolution in the form of the human element would have remained on earth. Man would have spiritualized himself in an entirely ascetic way and would have entered into the spiritual luciferic world in this ascetic spiritualization, leaving behind the corporeal. Human souls would have found their salvation, but the earth would have remained purposeless. The bodies of human beings would never have been able to render the service to the souls that they really ought to render. To prevent this constitutes the significance of the Mystery of Golgotha.

We must now look back once more to the evolution before the Mystery of Golgotha if we wish to understand this matter completely. From the very beginning of the evolution of the earth, it was Lucifer's intention to lead men away from the earth into his spiritual kingdom. He had no interest in the rest of earthly evolution but wanted only to possess what the higher gods had initiated in connection with man. He wished to lead this away in the form of the soul from the earthly evolution after it had remained for a time in the earthly form that comes from the exusiai, the spirits of form. In other words, he wished to lead the souls away and leave the earth to its fate. Why is it, then, that human beings did not follow this endeavor of Lucifer, before the Mystery of Golgotha, to lead them into a luminous world? Why didn't they? You may understand the reasons from many suggestions I have given here, even in these very lectures. They did not follow Lucifer because something was introduced into the evolution of the earth by the higher gods that prevented them from becoming light enough to do so.

As I have shown you, what is called the eighth sphere was introduced into earthly evolution in ancient times. As one of its aspects, the eighth sphere consists of man's acquiring such a preference for and attachment to his lower nature that Lucifer is not able to remove the higher nature from it. Every time Lucifer endeavored to spiritualize human beings, they were too strongly habituated to the flesh to follow him. If they had not been possessed by this cleaving to the flesh, to the physical nature, they would have followed Lucifer. This is one of the great mysteries of cosmic existence, that a divine element was actually implanted in human nature so that it might have, as it were, a greater heaviness than it would have possessed if this divine and necessary element had not been implanted in it. If it had not been implanted, human souls would have obeyed Lucifer. When we go back into ancient times, we find everywhere that the religions lay emphasis on the necessity of human beings reverencing what is earthly, what is an earthly connection living in flesh and blood so that they may be heavy enough not to be led out into the universe. Since all things having a relationship to both the human and the cosmic require not only an earthly, but also a cosmic arrangement, what you find described in my *Occult Science* occurred. At a certain time, as you know, not only was the earth formed, revolving in its orbit around the sun, but it was provided with the moon as its satellite.

What does it mean that the earth has a moon as its satellite? It means nothing more than that it acquired a force through which it can attract and hold the moon nearby. Should the earth not possess this power to hold the moon, then the spiritual correlative of this force would not be able to chain man to his lower nature because this force, from the spiritual point of view, is the same as that with which the earth attracts the moon. It may be said, then, that the moon is placed in the universe as an opponent of Lucifer in order to hinder him. I have already alluded to this mystery[120] and pointed out that in the period of materialism of the nineteenth century, this truth has been exactly reversed in Sinnet's book, *Esoteric Buddhism*.[121] There the moon is described as something actually hostile to man. The truth is that it is not hostile to him but prevents him from falling victim to the temptation of Lucifer; it acts as the cosmic correlative of what constitutes the attachment of the human being to his lower nature. Rather than tearing the souls out of the lower nature and thereby preventing its concomitant spiritualization, a subconscious process was required. Had the arrangement been conscious, man would have followed the urges of his lower nature in full consciousness and would have sunk to the animal level. There had to be something in the lower nature of which man was not conscious and which he did not follow except as a human being on earth would follow what flowed into his lower nature as a divine element. Especially the God of the Old Testament, the Jahve God, was concerned that the human being should remain on earth. Jahve is connected in this mysterious way with the moon, as you will find explained also in *Occult Science*. From this statement you can estimate how materialistic it was to designate the moon as the eighth sphere, whereas it really is the force itself, the sphere, that attracts the moon. In her misguided ways, Blavatsky developed special malice in her *Secret Doctrine* by maligning the Jahve God as a mere moon god. She wanted to replace him with Lucifer whom she undertook to represent as the friend of the spirit. To be sure, Lucifer is just that, but only in the particular sense I have explained. Blavatsky tried to represent the Jahve God as the god of the mere lower nature, whereas what really constituted an opposition to Lucifer was implanted in the lower nature.

You see how dangerous it is to set up truths that may be perverted to their opposite. Blavatsky was misled by certain beings who had an interest in guiding her into putting Lucifer in the place of Christ, and this was to be achieved by introducing precisely the opposite of the truth of the eighth sphere and by maligning the Jahve God, representing him merely as the god of the lower nature. Thus did those cosmic powers who desired to advance materialism work even through what was called "theosophy." Materialism would obviously have sunk to its worst abyss if men had come to believe that the moon was really the eighth sphere in the sense indicated by Sinnet or Blavatsky, and that Christianity must be fought in every way.

Now, placing the opponent of Lucifer in the lower nature of man was only possible so long as the human being had not developed his ego in the manner in which this took place at the time of the Mystery of Golgotha. The degree to which this ego was subdued in ancient times is greatly underestimated. It was subdued and appeared only during the centuries just prior to the Mystery of Golgotha. Then it no longer sufficed merely to place in the subconscious, or unconscious, nature what strove against Lucifer. Something had to come that the human being could take up into his consciousness; this is the Christ, who follows the Jahve God in evolution. It was necessary that the Christ should come so that through an avowal of Him the human being might consciously oppose mere spiritualization as this was striven for on the part of Lucifer. Christ descended for all human beings and only through our feeling related to everyone else do

201

we belong to the earth. The deeper understanding of the Christ derives from our connection with all human beings and from our effort to attain a full and complete connection with them.

You see, as long as men lived without the fully developed ego before the Mystery of Golgotha, they passed through the portal of death into the spiritual world and entered into relationship with archai, archangels and angels. But since they had not yet developed the complete ego here on earth, even after they had passed through the portal of death they did not need to develop a connection with the higher spiritual beings consciously. This was regulated through the atavistic powers that lay within them. But since the Mystery of Golgotha—not by reason of it but since that time—everything has become quite different. Let us look at ourselves and see how things have changed.

A human being passes through the portal of death as do others or perhaps one person passes through the portal of death and others remain here on earth. By virtue of his or her passing through the portal of death, an individual continues to be a human being and if we desire to keep our connection with such an individual, our relationship to him or her cannot change. Let us now bear in mind, however, that at the present time, since we live after the Mystery of Golgotha, the human being in ascending into the spiritual worlds passes through the hierarchies of the angels, archangels, and archai. Since he is now within the period in which his ego has developed here on earth, he possesses a consciousness also for the other hierarchies that are above them. That is to say, he develops consciously the forces poured into him from beings that are even higher than the archai. What does this signify? Let us take a concrete case and assume that through death a person loses one who is dearly beloved. The one who has passed through the portal of death maintains for many years, of course, the connection with certain inclinations and tendencies that he had during his lifetime. However, since he developed his ego here in his lifetime as a human being, something in him begins consciously to work on the perspective of his next incarnation immediately after he has passed through the portal of death. This occurs in a decisive way in what I have called in the Mystery Plays,[122] the midnight of existence; it appears to some extent in human consciousness immediately after death. When a person is in this state, however, there lives in him what already draws him away from what he was born into in his last life. Let us suppose that in his last life he belonged to a certain nation. The person who has remained behind continues to belong to this nation in his physical body, but a force belonging to an entirely different nation takes possession of the one who has died. How can the bond between the two continue beyond death undiminished in strength? Only when the one who remains here has an understanding for what extends above the angels, archangels and archai; that is, above what one may develop here through one's inclination toward relationships to human groups. If someone remains behind as a member of a certain nation and loses a friend through death who is already preparing to be a member of a different nation, the bond of love with the dead person cannot remain undisturbed. Only through the fact that both confess Christ, that they understand Christ in what extends above all differentiations of men can this bond be supramundane. What did John the Baptist say when Christ Jesus came to him to be baptized? "Behold, the Lamb of God, who beareth the sins of the world." The full significance of these words might make us grow pale were we to take it in its full weight.

It may be asked why Christ has been victorious and not Mithras. During the time when Christianity was spreading from the East toward the West, the Mithraic cult expanded along the Danube all the way to France and Spain in Western

Europe. The cult of Christ, however, has been victorious over the Mithraic cult. Why? Because the cult of Mithras had developed from extending above angels, archangels, and archai, and through this upward extention wished to attain to the Light-giver and Ruler of the World. What is the Christ in contrast to this? The Christ is He who took upon Himself for the evolution of the earth all that is bound up with angels, archangels, and archai; that is, all that chains man to the earth. He bears the sins of the world, those sins that have come into the world through human differentiation. He is a being in whose presence we must say, "I belong to a single human community, but because I belong to a single human community, to something connected with the earthly, I separate myself from the divine. From this I can be redeemed only by a Being who has nothing to do with human differentiation. The Christ in me leads me beyond earthly differentiations, teaches me to feel that what has been produced by earthly differentiation is suffering, that it brings death. Only through such an understanding of the Christ in me do I find my connection with the spiritual world." All that entered humanity through the fact that differentiations have come about has been removed from it through the entrance of Christ into the world. Christ could not, therefore, be a divinity like Mithras, who guides the human being beyond himself. He is the one God who descended to earth and took away the sins of differentiation and cleansed man of them. Mithras rushes through the world with a sword in his hand that he thrusts into the lower nature to slay it; under him the lower nature dies. Christ offers Himself as the Lamb of God, who takes the lower nature into Himself in order to redeem it.

Much lies in this comparison, immeasurably much! It is for this reason that the idea of Christ is not to be separated from the idea of death and resurrection. Only when we realize that what leads man to the earth brings him death, that there is more in him than what brings him into the earthly atmosphere, and that something is in him that is the Christ Who leads him away again: *In Christo morimur*—only then do we understand the Christ and know that we are united with Him. Thus, the representations of the ancient gods could set triumphant beings before us, but the Christ could only be presented by the joining of human beings in suffering and death because Christ endured all that enters into the differentiations of man throughout the earth. It is thus that Christ becomes the One Who leads man through death and back into the spiritual world, but this also makes Him the Divinity Who may be approached here on earth as we pass beyond maya or illusion. As the Christ is born here from the womb of maya, so must we draw near to Him by advancing beyond maya and appealing to Him in all the higher reality that projects into maya, but isn't maya itself.

If it is to turn to this worship of Christ, mankind will still need a long time on earth. Nevertheless, we must begin again to take Christianity earnestly. It is taken least of all seriously by the theologians who are frequently in conflict over whether or not Christ performed miracles and, for example, drove out demons through them. Well, it is entirely superfluous to argue over whether or not Christ drove out demons. It is more important that we learn to reproduce His miracles and thereby cast the demons out now where we can. We still have little power to cast out demons in the higher sense as antiquity knew how to do through its atavism. That is the destiny, the karma, of our epoch. But we can begin to drive out those demons of whom I spoke yesterday; they are there and it is negative superstition to suppose that they are not. How do we drive them out? Humanity will be convinced that they are being driven out when what is unholy service today becomes holy; that is, permeated with the Christ consciousness. In other words, this means that we must change to a sacramentalism in which man's deeds are imbued by the consciousness that the Christ stands behind him everywhere. Thus, he ought to do nothing in the world except that in which the Christ can help him. If he does something else, the Christ must also help him but He is thus crucified again and again in human deeds. The crucifixion is not merely a single deed; it is a continuing deed. So long as we do not drive out the demons through what lives in our souls by changing external mechanical actions into holy actions, we will continue to crucify Christ. It is from this point that our education to a true Christianity must begin. What was symbolically practiced in the ancient cults of Christianity and was once performed only on the altar must take hold of the entire world. Humanity must learn to deal with nature as the gods have done; it should learn not to construct machines in an indifferent way but to fulfill a divine service and bring sacramentalism into everything that is produced.

It is already possible to make a beginning in many things. Most of all, human beings can begin to develop sacramentalism in two areas. The first is that of educating and teaching children. We will begin to spiritualize what the religions call "baptism" when we look upon every human being who enters the world through birth as bringing his/her Christ forces with him/herself. Thus we will have the right reverence before the growing human being and can then direct the entire education and especially the teaching of the child in this spirit so that we bring in this teaching a sacramentalism to fruition. We can achieve the same end when we not only look upon educating and teaching the child as a divine service, but also *make* it such a divine service. Finally, when we endeavor to bring what we call our knowledge into our consciousness in such a way that, as our souls are filled with ideas of the spiritual world, we are aware that the Spiritual world is entering into us and that we are being united with the spiritual; when we look upon that as a "communion"; when we can realize true knowledge in a sentence you find expressed before 1887: "Thinking is the true communion of humanity,"[123] when the symbolic sacrament of the altar will become the universal sacramental experience of knowledge. It is in this direction that the Christianizing of man must move forward. You will then come to the knowledge that, everywhere in life, reality enters into maya in everything that is related to the Christ, and that to look upon reality after the manner of modern science with its world conception is in the most eminent sense unchristian.

It is strange how people nowadays are so easily able to adjust to what is unchristian and how little they can find their way to everything in Christianity that is appropriate to our time. As yet, we can see very little that counteracts materialism from, as I might say, a darkling inclination. If there are some beginnings, people embracing them proceed on false paths in that they, in a confused way, turn to old relations rather than to spiritual science.

Forgive me if I mention in this connection something that concerns me personally, but I am doing this only to cite an example. I may already have pointed out in these lectures that Hermann Bahr,[124] a contemporary personality whom I knew very well in my youth, is again in the process of seeking spiritual things. He is not seeking them in spiritual science because his interest for it is very limited. Take his very fine and intelligent book on expressionism and you will discover that he has only a marginal interest in spiritual science. But you can also see from the book itself that up to its publication he has informed himself about spiritual science only to the extent of his having read Levy's book[125] on my world view and on the people who oppose it. He has not found the way yet to really engage himself more deeply. However, it is interesting that he wrote a novel whose hero becomes acquainted with everything: contemporary chemical laboratories and so on, attending Oswald's[126] lectures in Leipzig, busying himself a bit with the theosophers in London, and so forth. His hero becomes exposed to everything which the present day offers in spiritual sensations, and he even dabbles in spiritism. And then he asks someone—I don't remember who it was—to give him esoteric exercises, which he practices for a while. But he is impatient, continues them only for a short time, does not achieve results and then abandons them; in fact, he gives up on all his endeavors after a short while. Then he has some strange experiences—the most interesting thing for me has been that, in a curious way, much in this book is reminiscent of what I have mentioned most recently in lectures, even about actual events, although I haven't seen Hermann Bahr for the past twenty-eight years except once, but then we definitely did not discuss questions related to our views of the world. Recently, Hermann Bahr also had a play of his staged which is entitled *The Voice*. One need not defend this play for the simple reason that Hermann Bahr just is not trying to find his way into spiritual science, which he finds too difficult, but is relapsing into orthodox, or let's say, more recent Catholicism. At any rate, he is in search of spiritual life.

It is interesting how the hero of this play is in search of spiritual life. He is married to a lady, the daughter of a very orthodox mother and herself very orthodox in view. This lady is deeply serious about Christianity—more so than can be expected of a human being. However, her husband, the hero of the play, is a disciple of Oswald and Haeckel and is quite a materialist. Since his wife and mother-in-law are serious Christians, they are, of course, pained by the fact that the husband is a disciple of Oswald and Haeckel[127] and does not want to hear anything about the spiritual world. The wife grieves so much about this that she dies. After her death, the husband, from an unknown dark feeling, frequently thinks his deceased wife is calling out one thing or

208

another to him. One day, in the sleeping compartment of a train, he hears the voice of his wife with special clarity. This almost makes him insane; when the train stops at a station he rushes out and behaves like a lunatic in what I believe was the waiting room of a station. The train went on without him, and later, it was demolished in a railroad accident. The injured people are carried into the station and then he realizes that he had been saved by the voice of his deceased wife; she had caused him to leave the train in which he would have otherwise perished. This was the first time that he associated the voice of his wife with the conditions of reality. I do not want to condemn this; I simply want to tell you what a contemporary human being commits to paper these days. The hero of the play, by experiencing this apparent miracle and the after-effect of this woman's being beyond her death, realizes that he has been saved by her and this causes him to reflect anew about the connection of human beings with the spiritual world. Later, his wife continues to communicate with him frequently and the ensuing intimate friendship between his soul and the soul of his deceased wife leads him back to Christianity in the truest sense, and he overcomes his materialistic world view.

Even though we do not need to defend this play as such, we see that there are human beings nowadays who strive to instill the view into life that a truth of the spiritual world can manifest itself in maya, the great deception. Only a clear understanding of Christianity will build the bridge between the life here on earth and the life that exists in the spiritual world. Quite a few people today have a need for this spiritual world but we must admit that their number is insignificant in relation to the large number of those people who are either mired in traditional religions—and thus have fallen prey to materialism even if they don't admit it—or whose lives are directly determined by materialism and who do not have a real connection with the spiritual world. As I said before, we need not defend Bahr's play but it can nevertheless direct us to this important realization: Whoever wants to understand Christianity in its deepest meaning must get beyond the problem of death. After all, the most interesting thing in this play is that it takes as its point of departure the relation between the human soul and the human body which transcends the portal of death. To be sure, there is a basic error in all these things: instead of being led to Christianity—for which process spiritual science, as we understand it, wants to make a real beginning—we are again led back to an individual religious denomination.

If human beings would only understand the Christ in the way I have indicated today—and if we may still continue to speak here, I will deal with this matter more thoroughly—if they could so understand the Christ as the matter has been explained today in only the most elementary suggestions, then the feeling and conceptions that are developed in regard to Him could be conveyed to all human beings. Christ did not die only for those who belong to some Christian sect, but He died and rose again for all mankind. We must not associate some specific religious confession with the Being of Christ, but every religious confession is to be brought into connection with Christianity. If all people would come to understand how to conceive the Christ as has been indicated, Christianity would spread over the entire earth because the revelation of Christ and the revelation of Jesus are two different things.

If we go as missionaries to foreign cultures, or even to people in our own lands, and wish to force upon them the worship of Jesus within a religious denomination, we will not be understood since the knowledge of these people extends far beyond what is brought to them by this or that missionary. I should like to know, for example, what a Turk would say if a modern Protestant pastor should try to convey to him his conception of Christ. This conception as it is dealt with by modern Protestant pastors holds that there was once a Socrates, and then one who was somewhat more than Socrates, the Christ, the human being, the special human being, but still the human being—or any of those confused things that are said today in modern Protestantism about Christ. The Turk would say to him, "What! You tell me such a thing and you wish to be called a Christian? Just read the nineteenth chapter of the Koran;[128] much more is contained in it about the Christ than what you are telling me!" In other words, the Turks know a great deal more concerning Christ Jesus than what the modern Protestant pastors are prone to present because the Koran contains more about Him and Christ is represented much more as the Divinity in the Turkish confession than in that of the modern Protestant. This is simply not realized because nowadays people do not often go so far as really to read the original religious documents; rather, they utter much superficial nonsense regarding all possible religions.

The Jesus revelation, too, will touch men in the proper way, but they themselves must attain its truth by their own power. They will be able to do this after having passed through a sufficient number of incarnations. Everyone today is to some degree prepared to receive the Christ revelation; this is a distinction that must be made. However, many forces are at work to suppress the real Christ revelation and genuine spiritual science. In this regard you need only to remember some of the things I previously mentioned regarding my characterization of various endeavors which lay claim to being occult.

And now I would like to conclude today's lecture, but not without offering a short supplement which, for definite reasons that will become apparent to you momentarily, should not be considered as part of the lecture itself. What I have stated thus far I have said without reservations whatsoever; but what I am about to add I shall have to formulate, at least for the time being, with certain qualifications. That is why I am presenting these additional remarks separately. If I mention them today, it is because I consider them somewhat important within the framework of the considerations at hand.

I had indicated earlier that materialism reached its zenith in the middle of the 19th century. During that time, the people who knew that spiritual life would always be necessary for humanity considered teaching mankind that our environment really contains spiritual beings and effects. But I had also indicated that the leading occultists in those days branched off into two groups. One of them maintained that mankind was not yet ready to accept spiritual things, while the second one was saying in the middle of the century that mankind was indeed ready to be exposed in an elementary way to the most important concepts of spiritual life.

This second group, which advocates the teaching and the dissemination of the doctrine, has been reduced to a tiny number of people. However, the anthroposophical movement subscribes to the belief that the dissemination of the doctrine, as it is practiced by us in today's activities, is important for the transmission of spiritual knowledge to mankind. This question was first raised in the fourth decade of the 19th century, but those who held this view were, in a way, outvoted. After that had happened, they agreed to chart a new course and adopt the practice of spiritism. These people attempted to show that spiritualistic media—individuals who can be considered psychics—are able to receive messages from the spiritual world and that it would be possible by these means to get in touch with the realms of the spirit.

I have characterized these things before, and I also indicated that this entire attempt was a failure. It was a failure because in contrast to what I explained in my recent speech in Bern, the people involved in the experiments were unable

212

to pinpoint the various stages of our connection with the dead. Yet, the people in question did not want to deal with that phenomenon and, thus, the entire attempt was unsuccessful. All of the psychics indicated in the most primitive and elementary way that they were in direct communication with the deceased persons, and people always wanted to receive direct pronouncements from some deceased person through these media. Please note, this is not to say that what passes through a medium in an experiment cannot in some way lead to a contact with a dead person. But it is another matter to decide whether or not this is an unconscious, a genuine, and a proper mediation, and whether the mediation is possible at all. Some entirely different results were expected from the experiments. The psychic media were expected to make people understand that not only sensuous, but also spiritual forces flow continuously into human beings. Moreover, the experiments were supposed to teach people that spiritual things were preferably to be sought in the immediate environment, and not in the announcements of this or that dead person.

Since the whole attempt has proven to be a blunder, the serious occultists withdrew from this spiritistic experiment, and mankind now has to pay for this in that the psychic media have been usurped by all kinds of occultists. The latter do not pursue purely occult endeavors, but they chart a course that serves some specific human purpose. I have often mentioned this before: The person who wants to be a genuine occultist cannot merely serve a specific human purpose; rather, he must serve general human purposes, and above all, he or she must never employ improper and incorrect means in order to reach any goals whatsoever. But what isn't called occultism these days! You could get a notion of this if you read the report of the last Theosophical Convention, which contained the speeches of Mrs. Besant[129] and Mr. Leadbeater.[130] In these speeches, the present situation is depicted as the big struggle between Lords of Light, on whose side Mrs. Besant and Mr. Leadbeater are naturally to be found, and the Lords of Darkness. In these speeches the opinion is expressed that any neutral person not taking sides with any of these opposite parties, or more properly, with Mrs. Besant's and Mr. Leadbeater's Lords of Light, is a traitor. But still other things were discussed in these meetings. Mr. Leadbeater, for example, related from one of his profound occult insights that Bismarck[131] was supposed to have gone to France before 1870 and established magnetic centers in the North, South, East, and West of France. During the 1870/71 war, these magnetic centers established by Bismarck had been at work, according to Mr. Leadbeater, because otherwise the war with France would have been lost. This is the kind of stuff people listen to in theosophical meetings! Yes, they do listen to it, and one can only marvel at this or do something more drastic when one learns such things are mentioned. But as I said, there are many kinds of occultism in our age.

Now that serious occultists have withdrawn from spiritism, it is important to keep in mind that the latter has been taken over by people pursuing specific purposes. And it is quite easy to do this. Please keep in mind what I want to say in this supplement: Spiritism originated from an honest attempt to find out whether mankind nowadays is ready to accept spiritual truths. Also, remember that the attempt was a failure and that all kinds of movements, occult brotherhoods, as well as individuals—especially from America—have attempted to manipulate the psychic media one by one for their own specific purposes.

Following all this, I now want to speak about a report that our dear friend, Mr. Heywood-Smith, gave to me yesterday concerning the book that deals with the experiences of Sir Oliver Lodge.[132] I repeat, I am relating this with every possible reservation because I only have a report in front of me; it, however, is revealing enough. I reserve the right to make further comments when I am in possession of the book itself. However, since I do not consider the matter unimportant, I would like to deal with it today. Should the report prove to be incorrect, I would, of course, clarify the things mentioned today. That is why I speak with reservations.

It is an extraordinarily significant fact, isn't it, that one of the most renowned scientific personalities of England, the great naturalist Sir Oliver Lodge, has written a book[133] containing things which, when accepted as he presents them, should be counted among the most significant pronouncements of the present time. We know, of course, that Sir Oliver professed in some of his other books that he acknowledges the existence of the spiritual world. But let me come to the facts:

Sir Oliver Lodge had a son by the name of Raymond who was born in 1889 and who, when the war broke out, volunteered for military service while Sir Oliver and his wife were in Australia. In March 1915 Raymond came to a vicinity of Ypern—and you can imagine how worried his parents were. Soon thereafter, Sir Oliver received a message from an American medium, a Mrs. Piper, which was dated August 15. This message from America had a peculiar content which, according to the report that I have in front of me, reads as follows: "Myers will take an interest in whatever fate has ordained for you and will protect you." However, this message was couched in the classical form of a poem by Horace. To repeat, Sir Oliver was notified by an American medium in August that Myers, formerly chairman of the Society for Psychical Research in London[134] but deceased fourteen years prior to the date of the letter, would protect and support Sir Oliver Lodge during a difficult event of which he, Sir Oliver, would be a part and thus work toward his protection. Please bear in mind that this message mentions only that Myers would help Sir Oliver during a difficult event.

Now, when Sir Oliver's son Raymond was killed in ac-

215

tion in September 1915, Sir Oliver at first related the message which had indicated that Myers would help him, to the death of his son. Subsequently, however, Sir Oliver's family was the subject of all kinds of pronouncements by the psychic media; in fact, several psychic media appeared on the scene simultaneously and delivered quite a few messages. Little by little, it turned out that all these messages had the following basic content: "Myers is united with your son"— Sir Oliver's and Lady Lodge's son, because seances were conducted with her as well. "Myers is helping your son, whose primary concern is that you receive word from him and, especially, that Sir Oliver should thereby be placed into a relationship with the spiritual world."—If one reads the various pronouncements of the individual psychics as presented in this report, one thing stands out everywhere. Throughout, the pronouncements exhibit interesting examples of psychic elevation; everything happens at a precise time; questions are being asked and so on, and they are then answered by the media. The whole process is extremely interesting. Even a picture of Raymond Lodge that was unknown to his family is found because the deceased son points to it and describes it, and it is then found in exactly the same place that he pinpointed. In short, in this book there seems to be compiled with extraordinary precision and exactitude all that can be experienced in many a spiritistic séance and which could lead to the events narrated. It is known that Sir Oliver had always been somewhat inclined toward these practices, much to the displeasure of his sons. However, after these happenings they became believers, too. Sir Oliver himself seems to have described in the most detailed manner how this bridge to his deceased son was constructed through the various psychic media.

What is important and what is presented is the fact that such a highly respected personality is induced to transcend into the spiritual world through the use of psychic media. I have to say this: From what I know abut the various séances, they themselves do not reveal too many new features.—But something else is very important. We have here a modern scientific personality of the first rank who, when writing in this fashion, can have a tremendous influence on the minds of human beings and who feels compelled to write in this way. That is very important because such writing influences many people and causes them to turn to the "media enterprise," which seeks to relate itself with the spiritual world in this fashion.

We are, of course, presented here with the same mistake of wanting to attain access to the spiritual world through spiritism which I previously described to you. But now let me ask you to look at the matter more closely. In the first message by the medium Piper which Sir Oliver Lodge received from America, a forecast is made of only one event against which Myers would protect Sir Oliver. To be sure, this event could have occurred in several ways. Suppose the son hadn't been killed in action. In that case, the statement that followed would have been quite compatible with the content of the message: "Well, you have been told that Myers protects your son in the spiritual world and keeps him from dying on the battlefield."—You will probably not doubt that the people in America could have known that Raymond Lodge had been stationed in an endangered zone of the battlefield and that, therefore, one could have made pronouncements similar to those of the old oracles: "Myers will protect your son." And had the son come out of the war unscathed, one could have said after the fact: "Myers did protect him by getting him out of the battle zone alive." Suppose, however, the son was killed in action, one could then easily relate the prophecy to Myers' role as a mediator in bringing father and son together from the spiritual world. Thus we can see that the original pronouncement was shrewdly phrased. The whole affair was contrived in

America. Since such fellowships extend, of course, over the whole world, the next medium was then put in touch with Lady Lodge. It is not necessary to know how such an anonymous session, as it is called in the report, comes into being. The procedures are as is customary in those sessions. But by now the sad news of the son's death had been received and Lady Lodge's psyche harbors all the after effects that such a message evokes. It is not difficult to demonstrate that what dwells in one soul migrated into another and communicates through the medium. Moreover, the son survived beyond death in the soul of his mother, in the manner that we are all acquainted with. Therefore, the accomplishment of the medium was nothing more than a rendering of what was already present in the souls of Lady Lodge or her family. This can be nicely substantiated from the protocol of the séances, which in each case is modulated to allow for the character of the major participants in these sessions. The name Myers is mentioned even by the media who were not acquainted with him. That, however, is not all that miraculous because Sir Oliver Lodge was a very good friend of Myers and had worked with him and so on. In short, everything would have been fine if only Sir Oliver, aside from the personal interest he took in his son's fate, had been content with carrying out an experiment whose sole purpose it was to show that there are spiritual effects in our environment. This was the original intention of the occultists, but then they abandoned this path.

I do not want to make judgments as I am sure the book itself will explain this matter, too. However, it seems we are confronted here with the obvious. Some people want to use Sir Oliver in order to attain definite special purposes. By using the constellations at hand, one very sorry occult brotherhood is likely to cite our case as characteristic when it makes its thrust to possibly, if you will, win over science to spiritism. Spiritism always likes to be considered as being "scientific," and it can be easily used to attain special purposes.

To mention just one example, the attempt had been made in another place in America to cure mankind of the idea of reincarnation. What took place? During the time when the events I characterized had already happened, that is, when the serious occultists had already left spiritism, a certain Langsdorff,[135] if I am not mistaken, organized all kinds of séances in several localities. When media were put in touch with the dead, the latter everywhere gave testimony that they were not at all waiting for reincarnation. And so the doctrine of repeated lives on earth was especially attacked in America. One can accomplish a great deal if one allows people to be approached in this matter by the pronouncements of the dead.

I wanted to discuss this matter quickly with you in a few words because I had talked about these things recently and because the example cited seems to be an especially good one. For how will the world be informed about this? The world will learn that a renowned scientist has confessed his allegiance to spiritism. Then, people will read the book, and most likely—we see this from our example—they will think that the case for spiritism has never been made so convincingly as in this book. As I said, I am speaking in this supplement to our lecture with qualifications because I reserve the right to come back to the matter after I have read the book myself. We are probably confronted here with an attempt by the so-called brotherhood of the left wing to attain special things by these very means. This may not be clear at first blush, but it is well known that there are numerous brotherhoods who wish to attain their special purposes in this fashion, and more is attained in this way than people are accustomed to believe. We will talk about these things some more later on.

219

Footnotes

Works of Rudolf Steiner that have appeared as part of the Complete Edition (CE) are listed with their bibliography number and with the year of the last published edition. See also the summary at the end of this volume.

1. These words are spoken by Faust's student Wagner in *Faust*, Part I, lines 570-573. The German text reads as follows:
   Verzeiht: Es ist ein gross Ergötzen
   Sich in den Geist der Zeiten zu versetzen
   zu schauen, wie vor uns ein weiser Mann gedacht,
   und wie wir's dann so herrlich weit gebracht.
   The German word "Ergötzen" connotes a passive and fleeting delight and is a contrast to the activating joy ("Erquickung") Faust experienced in line 568. Wagner's conclusion in line 573 symbolizes the shallow optimism of the materialistic Enlightenment. Wagner himself is incapable of true spiritual perception.
2. Svante Arrhenius (1859-1927), Swedish physicist, chemist, and astronomer, was the author of *Die Vorstellungen vom Weltgebäude im Wandel der Zeiten* [Conceptions of the Structure of the World in the Changing Course of the Ages] (Leipzig, 1908). The foreword of this book contains the quote from *Faust*.
3. See Goethe's *Poetry and Truth*, IV.
4. Johann Christoph Gottsched (1700-1766) was a writer and a Professor of Literature in Leipzig. He is best known for his efforts to reform the German theater and for having established rules for drama that conformed to French models.
5. Gotthold Ephraim Lessing (1729-1781) was the foremost poet and critic of the German Enlightenment.
6. Christian Fürchtegott Gellert (1715-1769) was a Prussian poet of the German Enlightenment.
7. *Faust*, Part I, lines 1-3. Faust reviews his past education and questions his knowledge.
8. The translation is from Walter Kaufmann, *Goethe's Faust* (Anchor Books: 1963), p. 95. This pronouncement in the third scene of Part

I, lines 382-383, reveals Faust's search for a cohesive spiritual force that holds the universe together. Later in the poem he admits that he has been seeking this knowledge through alchemy.

9. Lines 384-385 in *Faust*, Part I; cf. footnotes 8 and 35. The German word "Samen" [seed] refers to a term used in alchemy, but it is not certain that the word "Wirkungskraft" [working force] does. Some scholars think Goethe invented the word.

10. Johann Gottfried Herder (1744-1803) was a famous German theologian and cultural philosopher.

11. Baruch Spinoza (1632-77) was a Dutch philosopher, a rationalist, and a monist. His *Ethics*, published posthumously in 1677, exerted a profound influence on Goethe.

12. In the introduction to *Goethe's Scientific Writings* I (1883), pp. LV-LVIII, Rudolf Steiner depicts Goethe's relationship to Spinoza. Fritz Jacobi helped to deepen Goethe's knowledge of Spinoza's philosophy in the summer of 1774. After Goethe and Herder had renewed their friendship in Weimar, the two men and Frau von Stein studied Spinoza together. *Goethe the Scientist* (New York, Anthroposophic Press, 1950).

13. William Shakespeare (1564-1616).

14. Pierre Corneille (1606-1684) established a theory of French tragedy. Jean Baptiste Racine (1639-1699) was a famous writer of French classical tragedy.

15. Heinrich Jung-Stilling (1740-1817) was a German physician and writer.

16. Emanuel von Swedenborg (1688-1772) was a Swedish natural scientist and theosopher.

17. Paracelsus, Theophrastus von Hohenheim (1493-1541) was a Swiss physician, natural scientist and alchemist.

18. The reference is to Goethe's relationship with the pastor's daughter, Friederike Brion (1752-1813).

19. Goethe received the degree of "Licentiate of Law," a title which in Germany was regarded as being equal to the doctorate. From then on, Goethe used the title, "Doctor juris."

20. Götz von Berlichingen (1480-1562) came from an old Swabian family. He became the leader of the peasant uprising in 1525, fought against the Turks in 1542, and against France in 1544. His autobiography was published in 1731.

21. The reference is to *Faust*, Part I, line 584: "mit trefflichen Maximen." Faust, in lines 575-585, replies to Wagner's remarks (cf. footnote 1):

My friend, the times that antecede
Our own are books safely protected
by seven seals. What spirit of the time you call
Is but the scholar's spirit, after all,
In which times past are now reflected.
In truth, it is often pathetic,
And when one sees it, one would run away:
A garbage pail, perhaps a storage attic
At best a pompous moralistic play
With wonderfully edifying quips,
Most suitable to come from puppets' lips.

The translation of these lines is by Walter Kaufman (cf. footnote 8);
he renders "pragmatic maxims" with "edifying quips."

22. *Faust*, Part I, lines 1972-1975, trans. by Walter Kaufmann.
Mephisto says to the freshman student:
The laws and statutes of a nation
Are an inherited disease,
From generation unto generation
And place to place they drag on by degrees.

23. Siegwart, a sentimental novel by Johann Martin Miller, was published 1776, two years after Goethe's Werther, and immediately became a best seller.

24. The reference is to Goethe's letter from Frankfurt to Countess Auguste von Stollberg-Stollberg, dated February 13, 1775.

25. Goethe's *The Sorrows of Young Werther* was published in 1774. One year later, Goethe received Duke Kark August's invitation to Weimar and arrived there on November 7, 1775.

26. Frederick the Great in *De la litterature alemande* (1780).

27. Karl August, Duke of Weimar (1757-1828), son of Duchess Anna Amalia.

28. Charlotte Freifrau von Stein (1742-1827).

29. This treatise was written in 1784 and was published in Jena in 1786.

30. Goethe's letter from Rome, dated January 28, 1787.

31. Goethe's letter from Rome, dated September 6, 1787.

32. *The Robbers* had been published in 1781. In his *Glückliches Ereignis* [Happy Event] (1817), Goethe writes: "After my return from Italy, where I had endeavored to educate myself to a more definite and pure understanding of all branches of the arts and where I did not care what in those days was going on in Germany, I discovered that some recent, as well as some older, poetic works were in high repute and had widespread appeal. Unfortunately, they included some

222

works that I found extremely disgusting such as Heinse's *Ardinghello* and Schiller's *The Robbers*."
33. Friedrich von Schiller (1759-1805) was a dramatist, poet and historian and is regarded as one of the greatest German literary figures.
34. Hermann Grimm in the 21st "Goethe" lecture: "When two superbly gifted men combine in common endeavors, their strength is not doubled but multiplied fourfold. Each one has the other invisibly next to himself. The formula would not read G + S, but (G + S) + (S + G). The strength of one accrues to the strength of the other."
35. *Faust*, Part I, lines 384-385. The German text reads as follows:
    Schau alle Wirkungskraft und Samen
    Und tu nicht mehr in Worten kramen.
    The Kaufman translation (cf. footnote 9) of this passage, although preferable as a whole, leaves "Wirkungskraft und Samen" [vital power and embryo seed] untranslated and renders the two lines as follows:
    Envisage the creative blazes
    Instead of rummaging in phrases.
    To do justice to Steiner's remarks, I have here used Ann Swanwick's translation of these two lines. (P.M.)
36. Emil Du Bois-Reymond (1818-96) was a physiologist in Berlin.
37. Cf. footnote 35.
38. Francois de Théas, Comte de Thoranc (1719-94).
39. *Vom Menschenrätsel*, Bibl.-No. 20, CE (Dornach, 1957), p. 155.
40. Julien Offroy de la Mettrie (1709-51) was a French physician and materialist philosopher who wrote *L'homme machine* (1748) and who was a friend of Frederick the Great of Prussia.
41. Honoré-Gabriel Comte de Mirabeau (1749-91) was a Jacobin revolutionary leader and a celebrated orator.
42. Georges Jaques Danton (1759-94) was one of the leading figures of the French Revolution.
43. Maximilien de Robespierre (1758-94) was the French revolutionary whose name is usually associated with the infamous Reign of Terror.
44. Goethe left Karlsbad on September 3, 1786, arrived in Rome on October 29, 1786, left Rome on April 23, 1788 and arrived back in Weimar on June 18, 1788.
45. The friendship between the two men lasted from the summer of 1794 to the death of Schiller on May 9, 1805.
46. Cf. Rudolf Steiner's remarks in "Der pädagogische Wert der Menschenerkenntnis und der Kulturwert der Pädogogik" [The

Pedagogical Value of the Knowledge of Human Beings and the Cultural Value of Pedagogy], Second Lecture of July 18, 1924, Bibl.-No. 310, CE (Dornach, 1965).

47. Goethe arrived in Leipzig on October 3, 1765 and left the city on August 28, 1768. His illness began the end of July, 1768.

48. Susanna von Klettenberg (1723-74), a well known Pietist, became Goethe's prototype of "die schöne Seele," [the beautiful soul] in his novel *Wilhelm Meister*.

49. Goethe left for Strassburg on April 1, 1770, and returned from that city to Frankfurt on August 14, 1771.

50 Karl Wilhelm Jerusalem (1747-72) was secretary of the Brunswick Legation in the city of Wetzlar. He committed suicide on October 30, 1772, with a pistol borrowed from J. C. Kestner, who was also a friend of Goethe. The tragedy is generally believed to have prompted Goethe to write his *Werther*, as if he wanted to vindicate his friend's action. Werther, too, borrowed a pistol from a friend to kill himself.

51. Cf. footnote 18.

52. *Poetry and Truth*, XI: "I perceived, not with the eyes of the body but of the mind, how I approached myself on horseback, yet wearing clothes—pike-grey with a little gold—that I had never worn before. As soon as I shook myself loose from this dream, the apparition had disappeared. The strange thing is that after eight years from this incident when I was travelling on the same road to pay a visit to Friederike, I was wearing the very same clothes I had dreamt about—not by choice but by coincident." The later visit to Friederike Brion took place on September 25, 1779, during Goethe's second journey to Switzerland.

53. This lecture was preceded by a presentation of the scene in Faust's study (Earth Spirit, Faust, and Wagner).

54. Ann Swanwick's translation of *Faust*, Part I, lines 575-579, with Faust speaking to Wagner. Kaufmann's rendering of lines 575-585 is given in footnote 21.

55. Sophocles (496-406 B.C.) wrote 130 plays, seven of which are extant: *Ajax, Oedipus Rex, Oedipus at Colonos, Antigone, Electra, The Trachiniae, Philoctetes*. Recently, fragments of a satyr play, *Ichneutae* or *The Trackers*, were also found.

56. Cf. footnote 1.

57. The scene was written in March, 1788.

58. *Faust*, Part I, "Wood and Cave," lines 3217-3234. The translation is by Walter Kaufmann.

59. The philosopher and physician Gustav Carus (1789-1869) wrote the

224

book *Vergleichende Psychologie oder Geischichte der Seele in der Rei-henfolge der Tierwelt* [Comparative Psychology or History of the Soul in the Order of the Animal World] (Vienna, 1866).

60. Carus concludes the passage with a note: "Horses have been observed to accomplish similar feats; in fact, I have seen canaries do the same thing, although not quite as completely."
61. Herman Bahr (1863-1934) was a Viennese writer.
62. Oskar Pfungst, *Das Pferd des Herrn von Osten* [Mr. von Osten's Horse] (Leipzig, 1907).
63. *Poetry and Truth*, IV, 107.
64. Hans Sachs (1494-1576) was a shoemaker who became known as the foremost "Meistersinger" in Nürnberg.
65. Jakob Böhme (1575-1624), a shoemaker in Görlitz, Silesia, is re-garded to have been one of the most profound mystics in Germany.
66. Steiner lectured in Görlitz on December 3, 1908.
67. Kaufmann's translation. See footnote 21.
68. I Corinthians, 1: 20: "Has not God made foolish the wisdom of the world?"
69. Rudolf Steiner says in the third lecture of "Weltwesen und Ichheit" [The Essence of the World and Selfness], Bibl.-No. 169, CE (1963) that the American Keely invented such a motor in the 19th century.
70. Oskar Hertwig (1849-1922) was an anatomist who served as the director of the Anatomical-Biological Institute in Berlin from 1888 through 1921. His book *Das Werden der Organismen. Eine Widerle-gung von Darwins Zufallstheorie* [The Development of Organisms. A Refutation of Darwin's Theory of Chance] appeared in 1916.
71. Solfatara is the vulcanic sulfurgas well near Pozzuoli.
72. Friedrich Theodor Vischer (1807-87) spelled his last name with a V, not an F, and Steiner stresses that fact in his lecture.
73. Franza Feilbogen, *F. Th. Vischer's "Auch Einer"* (Zurich, 1916).
74. Max von Eyth (1836-1906) was an engineer and author of the book *Hinter Pflug und Schraubstock* (Behind Plough and Bench-Vice]. He introduced the steam-plough that was developed by John Fowler to Egypt, America, and Germany.
75. The "Ludolf number" was named after the mathematician Ludwig van Ceulen (1540-1610).
76. Henry Steel Olcott (1832-1907).
77. Dr. Max Burckhard (1854-1912). The description is based on Her-mann Bahr's *Erinnerung an Burckhard* [In Memory of Burckhard] (Berlin, 1913). Cf. Rudolf Steiner, "Gesammelte Aufsätze zur

225

Dramaturgie" [Collected Essays on Dramaturgy], Bibl.-No. 29, CE (Dornach, 1960), p. 60 ff. ("The Crisis of the Vienna Burgtheater").

78. Alfred Freiherr von Berger (1853-1912) was a theater manager, first in Hamburg and then in Vienna. On December 14, 1915, Rudolf Steiner spoke in detail about the novella *Hofrath Eysenhardt* in the fifth lecture of the cycle "Schicksalsbildung und Leben nach dem Tode" [The Formation of Destiny and the Life after Death], Bibl.-No. 171, CE (Dornach, 1964).

79. Lecture of October 30, 1916, published in *Innere Entwicklungsimpulse der Menschheit* [Inner Development Impulses of Mankind], Bibl.-No. 171, CE (Dornach, 1964).

80. The archai are the spirits of the time. "Arché" is the singular of "archai."

81. Printed in: *Luzifer-Gnosis 1903-1908*, Bibl.-No. 34, CE (1960) and as a separate edition.

82. The lecture was given on October 16, 1916, and was entitled "Das menschliche Leben vom Gesichtspunkte der Geisteswissenschaft (Anthroposophie)" [Human Life from the Point of View of Spiritual Science (Anthroposophy)]. It is printed in: *Philosophie und Anthroposophie. Gesammelte Aufsätze 1904-1918* [Philosophy and Anthroposophy. Collected Essays 1904-1918], Bibl.-No. 35, CE (Dornach, 1965).

83. Cf. Lecture V of November 13, 1916.

84. The reference is to lectures on October 7 and October 14, 1916, published in *Innere Entwicklungsimpulse der Menschheit* [Inner Developmental Impulses of Mankind], Bibl.-No. 171, CE (Dornach, 1964).

85. Lecture of October 29, 1916, "Innere Entwicklungsimpulse der Menschheit" [Inner Developmental Impulses of Mankind], Bibl.-No. 171, CE (Dornach, 1964).

86. John Stuart Mill (1806-73), British philosopher and economist, espoused a modified humanitarian utilitarianism but is also regarded by some as one of the founders of positivism.

87. Alexander Ivanovich Herzen (1812-70) was a Russian writer and revolutionary. Steiner refers to Herzen's work *Last Things and First Things* (1864) and quotes from Dimitri S. Merezhkovsky's book *Der Anmarsch des Pöbels* [The Advance of the Mob] (Munich, 1907).

88. Dimitry Sergeyevich Merezhkovsky (1865-1941) was a renowned Russian critic and novelist who spent nearly half of his life in exile in Paris.

89. See footnote 82.

90. Helena Petrowna Blavatsky (1831-91). Together with Colonel Henry Steel Olcott she founded the Theosophical Society in the year 1875 in New York.

91. Steiner did this in detail in the lectures he gave in the fall of 1915. Cf. "Die okkulte Bewegung im 19. Jahrhundert und ihre Beziehung zur Weltkultur", Bibl.-No. 257, CE (Dornach, 1969). *The Occult Movement in the Nineteenth Century*, (London, Rudolf Steiner Press, 1973).

92. Franz Ferdinand, Archduke of Austria-Este (1863-1913) was assassinated in Sarajevo on June 28, 1914.

93. The newspaper referred to was *Paris-Midi*. Cf. the speeches by Jean Jaurès published by Victor Schiff (Berlin, 1919).

94. *Almanach de Mme de Thèbes* [pseudonym of an alleged Mme Anne Victoire de Savigny, died in 1917), "Conseils pour etre heureux" (Paris, 103 ff.).

95. Cf. "L'assassin," in Almanach de Mme de Thèbes 1913 (Paris, 1912): "The one who is supposed to rule Austria (Franz Ferdinand) is not going to rule but rather a young man who at this time is not intended to be the ruler (Karl I)."

96. See "Més predications de l'an passé," *Almanach de Mme de Thèbes 1914* (Paris, 1913): "The tragic event that I predicted for the Austrian imperial family has not yet occurred, but it will definitely take place before the first half of the year has elapsed."

97. The reference is to Dr. Friedrich Mahling, Hamburg. In his lecture on October 26, 1916, in St. Gallen, Rudolf Steiner quotes from Mahling's booklet *Die Gedankenwelt der Gebildeten* [The World of Thought of the Educated]. Cf. *Die Verbindung zwischen den Lebenden und den Toten* [The Connection between the Living and the Dead], Bibl.-No. 168, CE (Dornach, 1976).

98. Jiddu Krishnamurti (1895-   ) was proclaimed by the Theosophical Society in 1909 as an incarnation of Maitreya, the messianic Buddha. After a two-year tour of America and England with Annie Besant, Krishnamurti renounced these claims in 1929.

99. Annie Besant (1847-1933) was elected President of the Theosophical Society in May, 1907.

100. Rudolf Steiner had been secretary of the German branch of the Theosophical Society since its founding on October 20, 1902.

101. Maurice Maeterlinck (1862-1949) was a Belgian writer.

102. Ku Hung-Ming, *Der Geist des chinesischen Volkes und der Ausweg aus dem Krieg* [The Spirit of the Chinese People and the Way out of the War] (1916).

103. pp. 168-169 in Ku Hung-Ming's book (cf. footnote 102): "Therefore, the first task must be to find some way to give the generals and politicians *power*, the power to make peace. The nations now waging war in Europe can achieve this only by tearing up their present Magna Cartas of Freedom and by replacing them with a new *Magna Carta of Loyalty*, such as we Chinese have it in our religion of the good citizen."

104. Confucius, Chinese Kung Fu-tse (551-579? B.C.), a Chinese philosopher. Lao-tze (born approximately 604 B.C.) was also a Chinese philosopher and the co-founder of Taoism. He was called "the old master."

105. This encyclical has become known as the so-called "Syllabus Pius' IX."

106. Prior to this lecture, a scene from *Faust*, Part I, had been performed: Mephisto and the freshman student.

107. Galileo Galilei (1564-1642). The letter is quoted from Angelo de Gubernatis, "Galileo Galilei," *Deutsche Revue* (March/April, 1909).

108. Cosimo I de'Medici (1519-74), Duke of Florence (1537-69) and Grand Duke of Tuscany (1569-74).

109. Johann Sebastian Bach (1685-1750).

110. Alphonse Leblais, *Matérialisme et Spiritualisme* (Paris, 1865).

111. Maximilian Littré (1801-81) was a philosopher, linguist, and follower of the positivist Auguste Comte (1798-1857).

112. Albert Steffen (1884-1963), Swiss poet and writer, became president of the Anthroposophical Society after the death of Rudolf Steiner.

113. Albert Steffen, *Der rechte Liebhaber des Schicksals* [The True Lover of Destiny].

114. Matthew 18:20.

115. Grimm made this statement in the 23rd "Goethe" lecture with reference to the Laplace-Kant fantasy of the origin and past destruction of the earth.

116. In 1711, the English inventor Thomas Newcomen (1663-1729), together with this associate Cowley, succeeded in constructing an atmospheric steam engine that could be used for practical purposes in 1712.

117. The Scottish inventor James Watt (1736-1819) was at first unable to utilize for his steam engine the already well known mechanism of the crankshaft and connecting rod because it had already been patented by someone else. However, he circumvented the problem by utilizing the so-called solar and planetary rotary motion.

118. *Von Jesus zu Christus* (Karlsruhe, 1911), Bibl.-No. 131, CE (Dornach, 1974). *From Jesus to Christ*, (London, Rudolf Steiner Press, 1973).

119. Matthew 25:40.

120. Cf. the lectures in *Die okkulte Bewegung im 19. Jahrhundert und ihre Beziehung zur Weltkultur*, Bibl.-No. 257, CE (Dornach, 1969). *The Occult Movements in the Nineteenth Century*, (London, Rudolf Steiner Press, 1973).

121. Alfred Percy Sinnett, *Esoteric Buddhism* (1883).

122. Rudolf Steiner, *Vier Mysteriendramen* [Four Mystery Plays], Bibl.-No. 14, CE (Dornach, 1962). *Four Mystery Plays*, (Steiner Book Centre, Toronto, 1973).

123. Cf. Preface to: *Goethe's Scientific Writings*, II, Rudolf Steiner, ed. (1887) in *Kürchner's Deutsche National-Litteratur*. Photomechanic reprint, 5 vols., Bibl.-No. 1 a-e, CE (1975). *Goethe the Scientist*, (New York, Anthroposophic Press, 1950).

124. Hermann Bahr (1863-1934), a Viennese writer who was the author of the book *Expressionismus*, 3rd edition (Munich, 1919) and of the play *Die Stimme* [The Voice] (Berlin, 1916).

125. Eugene Levry, *Rudolf Steiners Weltanschauung und ihre Gegner* [Rudolf Steiner's World View and its Opponents] (Berlin, 1913).

126. Wilhelm Oswald (1853-1932) was a chemist.

127. Ernst Haeckel (1834-1919) was a renowned zoologist.

128. The nineteenth sura of the Koran is entitled "Mary."

129. Cf. footnote 99.

130. Charles Webster Leadbeater (1847-1934) was a prominent personality in the Theosophical Society.

131. Otto Fürst von Bismarck (1815-1898) was the Prussian Chancellor who founded the Second German Empire in 1871.

132. Oliver Lodge (1851-1940) was an English physicist and a member of the Royal Society.

133. Oliver Lodge, *Raymond, or Life and Death* (1916).

134. Frederic W. H. Meyers (1843-1901), a spiritist and friend of Sir Oliver Lodge, was a co-founder of the Society for Psychical Research in London.

135. Georg von Landsdorff was a physician who had previously lived and worked in Freiburg i.Br.

A Note on the Transcription of Lectures

From Rudolf Steiner's Autobiography
The Course of My Life, XXXV (1925)

My anthroposophical work has yielded two results: first, the books I have published for all the world to read; secondly, a number of lecture courses which were at first intended for private printing and were to be for sale only to members of the Theosophical (later the Anthroposophical) Society. These were reports of my lecture, more or less accurate, which I did not have the time to correct. I would have preferred oral pronouncements to have remained just that, but the members wanted a private printing of these courses and that is what was done. Had I had the time to correct the transcriptions, the restriction "for members only" would have been unnecessary from the very beginning. Now, for more than a year, the restriction has been omitted anyway.

Here, in *The Course of My Life*, it is above all necessary to state how the published books and the privately printed material combine into what I developed as anthroposophy.

Whoever wants to trace my inner struggles and see how I worked to acquaint contemporary consciousness with anthroposophy must do so on the basis of publications that were intended for the general public. It is in them that I dealt with everything that in our time qualifies as the search for knowledge. The reader will find in these works what increasingly took form within me through "spiritual perception" and what became—albeit incompletely in many ways —the edifice of anthroposophy.

One requirement that emerged was to build "anthroposophy" and thereby respond to the need of imparting information from the spiritual world to the generally educated public of our time. Soon, however, it also became necessary to fully address what from within the membership revealed itself as spiritual needs and intellectual longings.

Above all, a strong inclination was felt to have the Gospels and the Bible presented in the light of what had emerged as anthroposophical inquiry. The members in the courses wanted to hear about the revelations that mankind had been given.

In response to this request, internal lecture courses were given which were attended only by members. They, however, were familiar with the rudimentary pronouncements about anthroposophy so that one could speak to them as one would to advanced students of anthroposophy. The approach in these internal lectures was different from the one necessary for the publications that were entirely intended for the general public.

In these inner circles it was appropriate for me to discuss the subject matter in a less structured way. If the same subject matter had from the outset been designated for public presentation, I would have had no choice but to rearrange things accordingly.

Thus, something is indeed present in the two endeavors, in public and private writings, which derives from two different backgrounds. The exclusively public writings are the result of what struggled and was at work in me, whereas in the privately printed material the society joins me in my struggle and labor. When it does, I listen to the pulsations in the soul-life of the members and as I vividly partake in what they have to say, the form of the lecture takes its shape.

At no time is anything whatsoever mentioned in the lectures that is not the clearest result of the developing anthroposophy and absolutely no concesion is made to accommodate the members' prejudices or preconceived notions. Anyone reading this privately printed material can accept its contents in the fullest sense as a pronouncement of what anthroposophy has to say. Therefore, when complaints in this regard became too persistent, we could without hesitation abandon the practice of distributing the printed material only to members. What will have to be accepted, however, is that the transcriptions not checked by me may contain some errors.

We will concede the right of judging the content of this printed material only to those who know what is acceptable as a prerequisite for making such a judgment. The *minimal* prerequisite for an appreciation of this printed material is that one has an anthroposophical understanding of man, and of the cosmos to the extent that its nature is explained by anthroposophy. Moreover, one should know "anthroposophical history" as manifested in the pronouncements from the spiritual world.

CPSIA information can be obtained
at www.ICGtesting.com
Printed in the USA
FFHW020730141019
55502997-61308FF